Cooking in Russia

YouTube Channel
Companion Reader

VOLUME 1

by
Greg Easter

Dedicated with boundless gratitude to

Gennady and Tatyana Bolshakov

Who made this book possible through
their gracious support and help in Russia.

TABLE OF CONTENTS

INTRODUCTION

This was written first and foremost to provide additional information to the video recipes online at:

www.youtube.com/user/cookinginrussia

Measurement Conventions

While many cooks use terms like teaspoon and tablespoon very loosely, that is not how professional chefs operate. A teaspoon (abbreviated with a lower case t) is 5 cubic centimeters, or 5ml. A tablespoon (abbreviated as an upper case T) is 15 cubic centimeters, or 15ml, or 1/2 ounce. Careful measurement means reproducible results, and it is the path to perfecting any dish.

Cookbooks

One of the questions that I am frequently asked is a recommendation for a great cookbook. When you are first learning to cook, good solid recipes such as the New York Times Cookbook will offer practical and useful advice on the basics. You don't even have to understand why the recipe works. You can just follow it robotically and you will obtain a far better result than you would have without a recipe, because you still at that stage where you lack the ability to make good decisions about compatible flavors, preparation methods and cooking times on your own. This is the stage that most amateurs never rise above, and that's okay! Not everyone who hammers a nail yearns to design a skyscraper.

However, for those who are more serious about cooking and have moved beyond the simple recipe stage, there is a gaping hole in resources. The vast majority of cookbooks are aimed at beginners. After all, amateurs comprise nearly the entire market, if we are to believe the research of publishers. So even when a distinguished restaurant chef produces a book, the content is invariably edited and simplified to help make it more saleable, because marketing people are convinced that there is no appreciable audience for recipes that call for 25 ingredients and require days of preparation—but restaurant recipes that evolved over decades are involved because they have been adjusted and modified countless times over the years. A cursory glance at almost any recipe will tell you right away how much effort has gone into optimizing it. The lack of this important middle ground between being an amateur and being a professional chef who attended culinary school, is the gap that I am trying to fill with my videos, and with this book. It is a stepping stone to you being able to successfully create your own dishes.

Developing Your Own Recipes

The key to successfully creating new recipes is not in trying to find things that no one has ever done before (you can't anyway, so don't kid yourself), but rather in selecting flavors and techniques that will produce the flavor you have in mind. It is very much like composing a symphony, and it has some of the same pitfalls.

The legendary orchestral composer Rimsky-Korsakov once observed that most composers go through the same early stages of development. Initially they fall in love with the string section, because when a sea of violins and cellos are playing, even a rather poor arrangement still sounds good because the audience is mostly hearing the beauty of the instrument rather than the music itself. The next stage is a love affair with percussion, because the low frequencies of timpani and high frequency noise of cymbals distract the ear and will conceal a multitude of compositional sins.

I see a parallel in the early stages of a chef. The first epiphany is to rely on the natural taste of the ingredients. By keeping things simple, you get to take credit for nature itself. The person isn't tasting your cooking. They are tasting the ingredient. Of course an orange has loads of citrus, and what could taste more like corn than corn itself? However, the act of obtaining quality ingredients is not what being a chef is about.

The next stage of development—the percussion in the orchestral analogy—is an infatuation with hot spices. Because if you make a dish sufficiently spicy, that's all you will taste. You can get away with a lot of bad cooking if you bury it in hot peppers. This is not to say that the cuisines of nations like India and Thailand are inferior, because there is always careful balance there. What I'm talking about is the tailgate cook who pours hot sauce over everything. Okay, that's a hyperbole, but you know what I mean.

This doesn't mean that it is bad to let ingredients shine with their own natural flavors, or that foods should never be super spicy. The key is not to rely on those things heavily as crutches.

RESTAURANT vs. HOME COOKING

Most people have never worked in the kitchen of a busy restaurant, and that includes most television celebrity chefs. The real world logistics of what is required to be able to get any set of random dishes from a menu that could easily have 50 items or more on it, out the pass within 10-15 minutes, regardless of how many other orders are simultaneously in various stages of production is a challenge that no home cook ever has to face. Take a moment to reflect on this. Imagine yourself in the kitchen with orders for various dishes streaming in every couple of minutes. Every dish that goes out has to be factory-like identical in taste, portion size and plating. How is this accomplished? There are three solutions to these problems.

A La Minute Cooking

This is the most straightforward approach. When an order for scrambled eggs comes in, the eggs are cracked and butter goes into the pan as it is heating up. If nothing is ordered, nothing is made. The downside is that the menu must be quite simple and limited to things that can be prepared within the amount of time that a customer is willing to wait (usually 15 minutes is regarded as the upper threshold). Most small diners operate this way.

Mise En Place Cooking

I'm calling it this for lack of a better name. This is how the vast majority of fine dining restaurants operate. All of the complicated dishes and sauces are prepared well ahead of time and reheated when orders arrive at the kitchen. This facilitates a larger menu, but at the cost of food being wasted since it is impossible to guess exactly how much of any item will be needed to satisfy orders ahead of time. You are always operating between two undesirable conditions - selling food that has been sitting around for days because that item hasn't been ordered for a while (by chance), or raising operating costs by regularly discarding and remaking items before they actually become rancid. Trying to avoid this situation by making fewer portions of menu items ahead of time means that waiters will have to inform customers that the kitchen is out of menu items routinely, which leaves a bad impression. The key to success in this type of operation is keeping the menu as small as possible, but management generally hates that approach, preferring instead to blame the kitchen for not magically having an unlimited supply of every one of the 80 items on the menu and never having any food spoilage take place. The reality is that it's impossible with this business model.

Jewel Box and Degustation Menus

There are two approaches that solve all of these problems, but they only exist in the highest caliber of restaurant at this time. The first approach is what is sometimes called a Jewel Box restaurant in which there is a fixed price menu that changes seasonally (or sometimes more often than that). The customer has a very limited number of options. They may be given a choice between two different entrées, or a vegetarian option. Everything else is left up to the chef, who bases the menu on the best ingredients available at the time. For a while I was the chef at a place where guests paid for their meal before they arrived, as one would purchase tickets for a show. There were only two seatings a night, at 6:30 and 9:00. Courses were spaced out over time. If a customer didn't show up, there was no refund. If they showed up late, they were only served the remaining courses during that cycle, or "performance." The benefit to this approach is that everything is guaranteed to be perfectly fresh, and courses may be quite elaborate since the kitchen already knows well in advance exactly how many of each item will be needed and exactly what time it will be served. As a customer, you are getting the best possible food that this restaurant can produce. For the front of the house, the arrangements are simplicity itself, since each seat is sold only once for a fixed amount of time. For the chef, it moves the challenge from just trying to keep up with the chaotic struggle of filling orders, to being able to focus on making the most delicious and elegant food possible. It is a win-win situation for everyone, but it is not what most customers expect at a restaurant at this point in history, of course.

COMMERCIAL vs. HOME STOVES

Asian Wok Cooking

One of the most challenging problems for duplicating certain restaurant dishes at home is the equipment itself. Restaurant stoves are generally much hotter than any home stove. This is especially the case in Chinese restaurants, where the burner under the wok may have five times the heat of your home stove set to maximum. This creates what the Chinese poetically call "the breath of the dragon", in which food can be caramelized on the outside without drying it out. For this reason most authentic Chinese food simply can not be cooked properly at home, unless you have invested in a special wok burner and have a good exhaust system over it that mimics a restaurant kitchen. This represents an investment of several thousand dollars, but it will open the door to a world of flavors you can not achieve any other way.

Making Pizza

A less serious, but similar problem exists for trying to make pizza at home. A commercial pizzeria oven may be as hot as 400°C (750°F). This temperature is nearly impossible to sustain for long enough to cook a pizza even using a charcoal grill stoked with mesquite. One trick that can be used is to bake the pizza crust by itself for a few minutes in your oven at the maximum temperature setting, then remove it and put on the sauce, cheese and other toppings before returning it to the oven to finish cooking. This produces a better result, but it is still not as good as what can be achieved with a hotter wood-burning oven.

Scaling Up Recipes

If the recipe you are making calls for caramelizing vegetables or meat, you can not just add more to a pan and have it work. When a pan is crowded, food steams due to the moisture being released by the food itself. The cold food added to the pan will quickly lower the temperature and you will get lackluster results. A commercial restaurant stove does a much better job of maintaining heat, but even then there is a limit as to how much can be properly browned at one time. The recipes that I have included here for Tomato Sauce and Pizza Sauce are examples of this limitation. You can not scale them up by very much on a home stove before the results will suffer considerably. If you need a larger quantity, you will have to use multiple pans, or do consecutive batches if you aren't comfortable with managing several pans going at once.

Reheating Foods

One of the best things about commercial restaurant ovens is that they feature steam injection. This heats foods up very quickly, very evenly. Plus, the result comes out moist and fresh, looking like it was just made from scratch. Such ovens consume a great amount of power and will turn any kitchen into a sauna if you don't have a powerful air conditioning system going at full blast at the same time. Finally, they cost more than ten times more than a home oven. You can put a tray of hot water in the bottom of your oven and allow it to remain long enough for the water to come to a boil, then turn on your fan assist (if your oven has that feature) to improve your results a great deal, though. This is something to keep in mind if you have a large number of guests to serve. Especially if you are reheating any sort of casserole dish. A temperature of 180°C (350°F) in a steamy oven with the fan running will produce a penetrating moist heat that will give you much better results than a microwave, and your oven can obviously hold much more food at once than a microwave can. However, it is still a pale comparison to what is possible with a commercial oven.

BROWN SUGAR

A package labeled "brown sugar" with no other designation is almost always refined white cane sugar that has had some molasses added back in with it. Dark brown sugar just has more molasses put back in. The reason for doing this is commercial standardization. It is the same reason that milk is separated into skim and cream, and then some cream added back to the skim milk to make the desired fat percentage of "whole milk". True natural brown sugars are very different in taste than the refined products, and once you experience what true dark brown sugar is, you will find a whole new world of flavor has been opened up for you.

Brown sugar is one of the secrets of many professional chefs. The average home cook would not think to add an exotic brown sugar to something savory like a gravy or a marinade, but take a cue from commercial food manufacturers here - sugar makes almost everything taste better, and that doesn't mean adding enough to make it perceptibly sweet, either. This is where the real strength of unrefined brown sugars come in. They let you add those rich caramel notes without turning your entrée into a dessert.

There are literally dozens of varieties of brown sugars around the world, though many are quite similar. Several types of brown sugars that every serious cook should be familiar with are:

Cassonade

Partially refined brown sugar from Brazil. Unlike commercial brown sugar, it is not a mixture of molasses with white sugar, but rather raw sugar in which not all of the molasses and natural plant materials have been extracted. The flavor is more natural and intense than commercial dark brown sugar, but not as intense as...

Muscovado

Sometimes known as Barbados sugar in Britain. Muscovado is said to be the darkest of all the sugars sold. The crystals are left to dry in the sun, and then pounded by hand, which leaves the maximum amount of plant material behind. It has a very strong molasses taste and a sticky consistency. The flavor is overpowering in large amounts, but when you only want a touch of sugary goodness this is often the optimum choice because it packs a real punch of flavor.

Jaggery, Panela and Rapadura

Juice is pressed out of sugar cane, date palms, coconut, or sago palms, then left to dry before being pounded. It is not centrifuged, but it is heated to 200°C during production. The flavor is somewhat like caramel or toffee. In India it is called Jaggery, and it is used extensively in curries (and often one of the ingredients that is not mentioned in printed recipes). In Columbia it is called Panela. In Brazil it is called Rapadura. There are quite a few other names for this same product in other parts of the world, too.

Palm Sugar

Especially common in Southeast Asia. This is sometimes called Coconut Sugar, but it is not made from coconuts. Palm sugar is produced in a similar way to maple syrup, by tapping and collecting the sap of various types of palm trees and then boiling it down. Then it is dried until it crystalizes, though it remains somewhat sticky. This is not a substitute for brown sugar. The flavor profile is quite different, and like all of these other sugars mentioned here, you should acquire them and taste them for yourself to gain familiarity with the range of flavors available to you.

Demerara and Turbonado

These are spun in a centrifuge and are often labeled as "raw sugar" in the United States, but this is a misnomer because most of the plant material has been stripped out. Turbonado has a slightly more honey-like taste, but it is subtle. In most cases you an substitute these for any recipe calling for white sugar to obtain better flavor. Do not use either of these as a substitute for brown sugar, though.

MSG

There are some never ending battles in the culinary arena, and the general public fear of MSG is certainly one of them. This fear has been shown time and again to be a product of human imagination in double blind studies, without exception. I know that I won't convince those who have already made up their minds, but I will try, never the less.

To understand why MSG is safe, you have to first examine what MSG actually is chemically. The diagram below is glutamic acid, which is naturally present in just about every meat and vegetable you eat, as well as being an integral part of the metabolic chain in your own body. If you could somehow become allergic to this (and you can't), you would quickly die because you literally can't live without it.

The molecule below is MSG, or monosodium glutamate. It is the sodium salt of the same glutamic acid molecule shown above. But glutamic acid normally exists in this ionic form (shown below) in your system.

The sodium atom that is pictured to balance the charge is no different from the sodium in sodium chloride, or ordinary table salt.

$$Na^+ \ Cl^-$$

So why am I belaboring this point? Glutamic acid is a very important ingredient that comes in many forms. Famed chef Grant Achatz has openly declared that MSG is the third most important seasoning, right after salt and pepper. The same love affair with MSG is common among many other top chefs, including Heston Blumenthal and David Chang, to name but two. You will never achieve the restaurant quality taste of many, many dishes without accepting the fact that MSG is a required ingredient.

However, if you are still unconvinced, then whenever you see MSG called for in a recipe, substitute 1/3 the amount of salt. At least that way the sodium balance will be maintained.

REFERENCES

www.firstwefeast.com/eat/grant-achatz-talks-about-his-love-for-msg

"Glutamate as a Neurotransmitter", (published by John Wiley & Sons, 2012), by Steven Mennerick and Charles F Zorumski, Washington University School of Medicine, St Louis, Missouri, USA

Reeds, P.J., et al. (April, 2000). "Intestinal glutamate metabolism". Journal of Nutrition 130 (4s): 978S–982S.

Meldrum, B. S. (2000). "Glutamate as a neurotransmitter in the brain: Review of physiology and pathology". The Journal of Nutrition 130 (4S Suppl): 1007S–1015S.

TOMATO SAUCE

One of the most frequent and bitter complaints that I received in the early days of making videos was based on the misconception that I was using some kind of premade packaged tomato sauce. I explained this dozens of times in the comments section, but it bears repeating. The term "tomato sauce" in restaurant kitchens generally means pasata. This is puréed, vine-ripened tomatoes packaged without preservatives, and it is what every quality restaurant uses. Tomatoes only have a short season even if you grow them yourself and it is almost impossible to get genuine vine ripened tomatoes in stores because they have to be picked unripe just to survive being trucked to the warehouse and then to the store. Generally speaking, the best tomatoes you can possibly get are the packaged ones from Italy.

Some argue that "real Italians" make their own pasata. Some do. Restaurants generally do not, and even if you make your own pasata and bottle it from your own vine-ripened tomatoes, the results are no better than what is commercially sold if you buy a good brand. You want packages that contain only tomatoes and nothing else. Two excellent brands are Pomi and Cirio.

The next step up from this are San Marzano tomatoes, but in restaurants they are generally considered as not being worth the extra cost. At home you can indulge yourself freely, of course.

San Marzano tomatoes are an heirloom variety, and the most famous plum tomato to come out of Italy. The best of the best are grown in the rich volcanic soil at the base of Mount Vesuvius in a region known as Valle del Sarno. They are grown under strict regulations and as such, have been granted DOP status. Purists consider only the DOP product as being "real" San Marzano tomatoes.

In practice, most of the San Marzano tomatoes that come out of Italy are grown in other regions, but are also of excellent quality. The crops are all picked by hand at the peak of their ripeness. Because of the close attention to quality, DOP San Marzano tomatoes are widely regarded as the best in the world.

PRESSURE COOKERS

The two advantages of a pressure cooker are:

> *1. Aqueous solutions can cook at up to 120°C (248°F) instead of being limited to 100°C (212°F) imposed at atmospheric pressure.*
>
> *2. Flavor components are trapped inside the vessel as long as you don't run it up to the boiling point where steam escapes.*

Foods cook faster in a pressure cooker because of the higher temperature, but the flavor that they retain is not the same as it would be from cooking the same food at atmospheric pressure. Higher temperatures promote chemical reactions. Some of those reactions may be beneficial, like the Maillard Reaction. In other cases, flavor molecules are being degraded at the higher temperature, causing them to either change flavor or lose flavor completely. For more about this effect, see my video, *#2 ORGANIC CHEMISTRY IN COOKING.*

We can try to limit this problem by pressure cooking only the minimum time required, but it is a balancing act. If you want to see the full extent of the effect, try leaving something in a pressure cooker for several hours at a low temperature (less than it takes for steam to vent). The result has acrid tar that is the polymerization of pulverized cellular constituents. Of course, some foods are more prone to being damaged under pressure than others.

Making Stocks

I find that making duck stock in a pressure cooker is excellent. For most other stocks I still prefer the old fashioned way of a slow simmer at atmospheric pressure, because the amount of cooking time it takes to extract flavors is well into the region that it takes to cause unwanted chemical reactions. Heston Blumenthal has been a strong advocate of pressure cooking stocks, but this advice comes with some fine print. First, he is running a restaurant where volume is vital and stocks that occupy precious stove real estate for 12 hours (or more) are the scourge of any kitchen. Getting them done quickly may color his perception of perfection. Second, he is using a type of pressure cooker that has very little in common with the type you are going to have. In a recent interview he stated that his pressure cooker cost as much as the house he grew up in as a child. Finally, he advocates it mostly for dark stocks (brown chicken stock, in particular), where the unavoidable Maillard Reaction is on your side. If you are making a white stock, then you are trying to extract a lot of flavor without browning anything. You can't do that at a high heat and pressure. Although, if you ever find yourself competing on a cooking show where you only have an hour, then making any stock in a pressure cooker is a time saver that will yield some kind of result—but it won't be your best work.

An Alternative to Braising?

In a word, no! It is tempting to think of a pressure cooker as a kind of time machine in which a braise can be carried out much faster than it takes in the oven. The reality is that it isn't that simple. Pressure cooking will break down connective tissue in meats rapidly, and it does a great job of keeping flavors locked in, but (big surprise) it does *not* actually speed the passage of time. There is no substitute for time. In a laboratory, a reaction that takes an hour at 200 degrees can't be completed in half the time by doubling the temperature. What happens instead is you get a lot of unwanted reactions and waste products. The same thing is true in cooking. The deep, rich flavor that you get with a very lengthy braise at a low temperature is not going to be achieved in a short time at a higher temperature, despite what some manufacturers tell you. As I have already shown in videos, pressure cooking is great for "sweating" the fat out of poultry, and for breaking down tough cuts of meat in a hurry before you do something else with them. For the most part, pressure cooking should be regarded as an intermediate stage of cooking, with only a few notable exceptions, such as Biriyani.

DRIED CHILI PEPPERS

Every chef accumulates a toolbox of techniques and ingredients over their years in the profession. This is one of mine. Now of course the use of dried chilies itself is nothing special, but there are two particular innovations here that are not widely known. The first is to dry your own chilies and store them in a sealed plastic box in the refrigerator. As I have said in several videos already, the flavor you obtain this way is like the difference between the black pepper that's been sitting in a shaker for five years and black pepper you just ground yourself from peppercorns. Not only the additional heat, but a world of flavor that is missing in the dried chilies you buy. The only exception being chipotle chilies that are sold canned in adobo sauce. Those are acceptable. For anything else, make your own.

The second key that I am letting you in on here is a type of sweet chili that you can dry yourself and use in dry rubs and seasoning mixes of many types. It brings a depth of flavor that is somewhere between that of a tomato and a red pepper, but with an earthy umami character that can transform the ordinary into the extraordinary. It is also good for mystifying people as to how you got this delicious deep flavor. You can think of it like super-paprika. Any of the following will work:

Super Shepherd (Italian Sweet Pepper), from Italy

Draky, from Eastern Europe

Antohi Romanian, from Romania

The latter is my favorite of the three. These should be ripe (orange to red in color) before you dry them. I refer to these as *dried sweet red chili peppers* in recipes. If you are able to grow your own, so much the better. The seeds of all of these are available inexpensively online. Within the United States, the only source I know for Antohi Romanian seeds is **johnnyseeds.com**. In the United States and Canada, try **stokeseeds.com** for the other two peppers, and in Europe a good source is **seaspringseeds.co.uk**, however these peppers are available in supermarkets in Europe.

When it comes to hot chilies, I nearly always use either green or red serrano chilies. These are very hot and must be used sparingly. The green ones are reminiscent of jalapeño chilies, but are usually hotter, depending on the specific crop. Red serrano chilies are a good balance between serious heat and good flavor.

For most other chilies, such as habañeros and jalapeños, and Thai chilies, etc., I use only fresh chilies. I have never found any advantage to drying those.

The drying itself is very simple. Put the peppers on a wire rack in the oven and set it to 80°C (175°F) with fan assist running and leave them there overnight. In the morning, take them out of the oven and leave them to cool in the open air for an hour or so. Now seal them in a plastic container and store them in the back of your refrigerator. They will keep indefinitely, but the flavor profile will gradually change. This isn't necessarily a bad thing, though. Some chilies start to pick up notes of dark chocolate, leather and licorice after a few months that make them absolutely divine ingredients for creating complex flavors. Just smell each chili before you use it to see how it has "fermented". You'll see that they are absolutely nothing like the dried chilies you can buy.

This is probably the most confusing word to spell in English:

CHILI - a type of pepper

CHILE - a country in South America

CHILLY - cold weather

CHILLI - a dish of meat and/or beans simmered with spices

Russian Culinary History

The history of Russian cuisine is one of the most curious and least understood in the entire world of gastronomy. For centuries its development was severely hindered by governmental regulations, superstitious religious beliefs, and widespread food shortages. This is not a history book of Russia, and so in order to remain focused on cuisine here, just bear in mind that there have been many tumultuous periods with massive food shortages, various military invasions, peasant uprisings, political unrest, and a government that was absolutely tyrannical at times—capped off by the Orthodox church that was dictating a narrow list of foods that could be eaten, and what specific ultra-simple recipes that could be cooked on each and every day of the calendar. Even restaurants in Russia to this very day must file "technology cards" with the government, to get permission for each dish that they plan to use, and inspectors show up to make sure that the approved recipes are being followed without any variation. These factors collectively impeded the culinary progress of Russia right on up until the late 1990's when the era of rigid Soviet control ended and imported ingredients began arriving in markets for those who could afford them. Still, it took until the mid-2000's and a growing middle class before Russians began dining out in restaurants casually and getting their first taste of foods that had previously been the domain of nobility.

It is a deep seated cultural belief held by the majority of older Russians that food is not something consumed for pleasure, but rather for physical nourishment. To emphasize the enjoyment of eating is seen as being in contradiction to man's spiritual nature. I realize that many Russians would balk at my brief summation here, but that's because it is difficult to appreciate your own culture. Russians regard many other nations to be "absolutely insanely obsessed" with food, because from their point of view devoting time and money to food is not something one does. Russian culture has been shaped this way over many centuries, and it is so ingrained

Traditional ancient Russian furnace stove.

that Russians are not even aware of it.

This attitude began to significantly change among younger Russians in the late 2000's, but now with the approaching economic problems ahead, culinary exploration may once again stagnate. Only time will tell.

What follows is a concise summary of the seven epochs that shaped Russian cuisine over the last thousand years.

1. Ancient Russian Cuisine (9th to 16th centuries)

The 9th century is somewhat arbitrarily defined as the birth of Russia. Legend says that in the year 862, Scandinavian leader, Rurik of the Varangians, crossed the Baltic Sea and began to unite cities under him. How many were conquered by force and how many democratically chose him as their leader is not really known. Within 20 years he had gained control over a vast region, including the important metropolis of Kiev, which was Russia's first capital. Today Kiev is the capital of Ukraine, which has been a major influence on Russian cuisine. Rurik was followed by Oleg, and others who all worked at expanding their domain. Kiev was the key trading hub between Scandinavia and Constantinople. In the year 989, Vladimir, who was the great-grandson of Oleg, found it necessary to establish an official religion in order to further unite the tribes under him, just as Constantine had done. Vladimir carefully considered several popular religions at the time, and eventually chose Greek Orthodoxy to strengthen alliance with the Byzantine Empire. It was said that Vladimir nearly chose the Islamic faith as the official religion, but decided against it solely because Islam forbids alcohol. Not only was drinking part of Slavic culture, but more important, the primary source of nutrition because black sour rye bread was made from fermented grains. It is the same fermentation that produces the mildly alcoholic drink known today as *Kvas*. In short, there was no way to ban the fermentation of alcohol without causing massive starvation, and a colossal peasant revolt. It has been said that this was the only known instance in history when food decided religion. Although it might also be technically correct to say that liquor decided the religion.

During this period, the church exerted tremendous influence over what people ate. Foods were grouped into two primary categories: Lent, or "fasting" days, and the rest for non-fasting days. Between 192 and 216 calendar days of every year were designated as fasting days in which people could only eat fish, mushrooms and vegetables. The other days allowed for meat, milk and eggs, but did *not* allow for fish, mushrooms or vegetables— there was not a single day in the year in which both of these things could be eaten at the same time, and consequently no recipes developed that combined Lent ingredients with non-Lent ingredients. Still more limiting was that almost every item had to be cooked and consumed on its own. You could not combine different kinds of fish—or even different varieties of mushrooms! This effectively prevented the development of the culinary arts. Because it was also forbidden to mix vegetables together (except in boiled soups), there were no salads. The idea of serving each vegetable by itself persisted in Russia all the way up to the 19th century—a thousand years!

The church published a "gastronomic calendar" each year that specified what foods could be prepared on each day. This calendar was taken as a direct commandment, and widely followed. While the rest of Western Europe was developing the foundation of what would eventually become today's modern cuisine, Russians were conditioned to think of food as a necessity rather than a pleasure. This kind of thinking still persists to this day among the majority of working class Russians, especially those outside of Moscow and St. Petersburg.

Late in this period—in the 16th century—there were many dishes, but most were very similar and quite simple. There was a standard way of cooking each type of fish, each vegetable, and each variety of mushroom. Foods were still cooked on their own, but now finally there were some spices available for the rich. Those included anise, coriander, bay leaves, black pepper, cardamom, cinnamon, cloves, saffron, and ginger. Onions, garlic and parsley were now available to everyone. Meat dishes were not common in this era and usually consisted of some small portion of beef or pork boiled in a soup. The meat would be taken out of the soup and eaten separately. In a country that was abundant with wild game animals, this seems bizarrely limited. There was a reason, though. It was simply forbidden to eat most meats, including rabbit and veal. There were severe penalties for violating this mandate, because the aristocracy owned the rights to all hunting.

Cooking at this time was done in masonry ovens that also doubled as the home's furnace. There was a chamber at the bottom where wood was burned, and a compartment above that in which a pot could be placed. This is very similar design to how food is still cooked in Tajikistan today. On top of the stove/furnace was a padded bed that was the warmest place to sleep in the house (usually reserved for the elderly or sick children). Heating conditions in the oven were either a constant temperature, or slightly lowering with time as the fire was dying down. Cooking was done in clay pots with lids, and lifted in and out of the oven with a cast iron metal bar. Because the food was cooked in these masonry vessels that were both very hot and very evenly heated, the results were something along the lines of placing a covered clay pot in a wood fired pizza oven. It is unique, but quite limited. To put this in modern culinary terms, imagine if every meal you had ever tasted in your entire lifetime had been cooked in an electric crock pot.

The oldest known cookbook of Russia was produced near the end of this era in 1547, by the chef of Ivan the Terrible. This book consists only of the recipe names and a general description of dishes with no specific list of ingredients, or proportions, or any specific cooking directions. What we do know is that the peasants and the wealthy were all eating the same basic foods. The only differences were the quantity of food on the table, the use of certain spices, and the variety of dishes served at any one particular meal.

2. The Moscow State (17th century)

The late 16th to early 17th century was a turbulent period of peasant uprisings compounded by invasions from Poland and Sweden. Despite this—or perhaps because of it—there was economic growth and the expansion of trade that created a new economic class of merchants. The exchange of goods also brought an exchange of ideas. New exotic foods were available in public markets to anyone who could afford them. New techniques of cooking were acquired, such as how to cure hams and roast meats (instead of only stewing them). Former Russian peasant dishes were being reworked with these new cooking methods and new ingredients. As a result, regional cooking styles began to emerge. There were distinct variations between Siberian cuisine, the Don River region, the Ural region, etc.

The expansion of the nation brought in the culinary traditions of other developed cultures. Perhaps most influential at this time were the Tartars, who introduced raisins and dried fruits, as well as melons and tea. Dried fruit remains very popular throughout Russia to this day, but combining meat and fruit is still generally avoided.

It was in this same period that the government seized control of the vodka industry. All vodka was now made by the state, and they actively promoted drinking as part of a healthy lifestyle—and as a medicine. This is where the Russian love of vodka was born. Of course there were hangovers, which led to immigrants from the Balkans and the East introducing Russians to new sour and spicy soups as cures for those hangovers. Eventually these soups became part of regular dining such as the cabbage soup, Schi.

As the 17th century continued, the disparity of wealth between peasants and merchants increased. For the first time in Russian history there were entirely different kinds of meals for wealthy people than the poor, rather than just more of the same foods as had been the case in the past. This seems to have been the first time in history when degustation menus became popular. That is, a myriad of small dishes served over several hours. These dishes were usually grouped by the type of food, such as one type of mushroom prepared six different ways, served sequentially as six courses. A wealthy person might have 50 different courses during dinner. The Czar would have 150-200 courses, each being ornately decorated, and the meal would take up to eight hours to consume.

This was very much in contrast with the earlier church teaching that food was to be simple and plain. The Czar's table influenced wealthy guests who attended, and they returned home to recreate their own version of this splendor. In turn, those invited to their table would be impressed and come away with a sense that food was something to be enjoyed. They also gained insight as to new ways that foods could be prepared.

Still, this was all done within the severe limitation of a culture that prohibited combining different meats or fish in one pot, or being served together on one plate. So each dish was still an individual type of food, even if it had been seasoned with exotic spices and cooked in a new way. The mincing, or even fine cutting of anything—meat or vegetable—was also forbidden. So even with the advances made during this era and the newly available foods, the art of Russian cuisine was still quite primitive by the standards of other parts of Europe.

3. Peter and Catherine the Great (18th century)

This period marked a sharp divide between social classes, and so also in cuisine. For the first time in Russian history, it became fashionable for the privileged elite to travel to other countries for the express purpose of tasting new foods. For unknown reasons, Peter the Great was particularly fond of the Netherlands, while other aristocrats were primarily visiting Germany and France. For the first time ever they were tasting foods that had been cooked on a stove instead of in a hearth. A stove enabled chefs to sauté and deep fry foods, instead of only baking and roasting. The Russian nobility were tasting new complex dishes with sauces, as well as vegetables and farmed meats that they had never experienced before. In short, they were suddenly exposed to the level of sophistication in cuisine that had taken centuries to develop. Russian cuisine had been trapped in the Middle Ages by all of the regulations and rules governing how foods could be prepared. Of course Russia also had to contend with a cold climate that limited the crops could be grown. Although exotic imported goods were available in this period, few could afford them. Aristocrats would return home after their travels with an increased dislike of the plain and simple foods that could be prepared by their Russian serf chefs, so they began to entice foreign chefs to work in Russia at very high salaries. This practice has lingered on to this very day, and foreign chefs in Russia earn much more than Russians.

After centuries of following rules that forbid combining ingredients, and the only means of cooking for most people being their furnace, it was simply impossible to find a serf who knew how to cook the kind of food that the wealthy elite had developed a taste for. By the year 1760, it was said that every single wealthy person in Russia had a foreign chef.

It was during this era that Peter the Great moved the capital of Russia from Moscow to Saint Petersburg, which was the port where trade ships coming from Europe would arrive at. Saint Petersburg was known as a cosmopolitan city, since it was constantly exposed to merchants and visitors arriving by ship. Peter wanted Russia to be more like the rest of Europe, and he felt that moving the capital to Russia's "gateway to Europe" was a good start. This increased the availability of imported goods, and put even more distance between the cuisine of the elite and the rest of the general Russian population.

4. Saint Petersburg (Late 18th century to 1860's)

Word of the new techniques of cooking that these foreign chefs had brought with them began to spread to others living in Moscow and St. Petersburg, but that comprised only about 20% of the population of Russia. There were quite a few cookbooks published in Russia near the end of the 18th century, but they contained very few Russian recipes. The wealthy minority who could afford cookbooks were generally looking for recipes from other nations, particularly France.

It was around this time that the legendary chef, Marie-Antoine Carême, made his historic visit to Saint Petersburg. The duration of his stay and the extent of his contribution remains debatable due to contradictory accounts. Russian culinary history gives him credit for major reforms, while the French downplay his involvement. English and American history regarding Carême's trip to Saint Petersburg seems to have been translated directly from the French account at the time, which was likely biased due to the tension between France and Russia shortly before Napoleon's invasion. Never the less, both sides agree that Carême is to be credited for some changes to Russian cuisine. His first suggestion was to stop thickening soups with flour, which had been a Russian tradition for centuries. Carême also advocated the use of yeast instead of the sour rye dough that had been in use since the 9th century. He expanded the idea of appetizers, which had been mostly the German style of various small sandwiches up until that time. Now there were small-portion dishes of all types in service as appetizers. It is unclear how many of the changes during this time were the direct result of Carême, and how many were from the French influence in general. Other changes that occurred during this period were the widespread introduction of stoves, the use of exact measurements in recipes, and the modern salad that finally broke

The actual dining room of Dostoyevsky, which is on exhibit in a museum in Saint Petersburg.

the 900 year Russian tradition of not combining different vegetables together on the same plate.

This love affair with French culture changed abruptly with Napoleon's invasion of Russia in 1812. A renewed sense of nationalism led to the attempt at recreating old Russian recipes by using the new techniques and equipment acquired over the last century. In 1816 a Russian nobleman published an important book on authentic Russian cuisine, containing many nearly forgotten recipes that he personally gathered by interviewing grandmothers and the oldest serf chefs that he could find. The book was the best attempt made at that time, but still inexact, incomplete, and only contained only a small number of classic dishes. The book itself was a success, but in reality French cuisine continued to be served on the tables of wealthy Russians, despite it being politically incorrect.

5. All Russian National Cuisine (1860's to 1910's)

Two fundamental changes to the socio-political landscape occurred during this period. The first was the abolishment of serfdom in 1861. This was even more important than the freeing of slaves in America, since it affected virtually the entire population! People were no longer considered pieces of state property that could be bought and sold, or simply killed without reason. This new freedom was cause for much celebration. Former serfs sought to improve their quality of life, and one obvious way was cuisine. Since they had not developed the same sophisticated taste for French cuisine as the aristocracy had cultivated over the previous century, the newly freed serfs went to work improving the quality of the peasant dishes they were familiar with, using better ingredients and better equipment.

The second fundamental change that took place in this era was the building of railroads. For the first time in Russian history, large numbers of people were able to travel and migrate. The regional cuisine of other parts of Russia spread back to Moscow and Saint Petersburg. One example of this was Siberian dumplings, known as pelmeni, which remain a staple food throughout Russia to this day. Because of the amount of travel done across Russia, cuisine became more homogeneous. By the early 20th century, every table across Russia had common dishes that included bread, pancakes, numerous common kashas, soups, pies (pirogi), salted and pickled vegetables and mushrooms. All of these foods were common throughout a nation that encompassed a sixth of the entire planet.

6. Soviet Cuisine (1920 to 2000)

The revolution of 1917 and subsequent formation of Soviet Russia brought dramatic changes affecting every aspect of life. The history behind the Iron Curtain was so highly politicized on both sides that has became difficult to separate fact from fiction in historical accounts. English language sources are often in stark contrast to Russian sources from the time. Both sides had an agenda that strongly colored everything written. Ask anyone over the age of 60 in Saint Petersburg what things were like, and they will describe an existence that is substantially different from both the Soviet and the Western accounts, often being fondly regarded as having been a better life for nearly everyone overall.

For the first time now, pasta and white bread became available to everyone. New soups that were made with meat stocks were introduced, including Borscht from Ukraine. Some of the other classic dishes that the West now thinks of as original Russian cuisine were actually imported recipes from neighboring nations that were swept behind the Iron Curtain for more than 70 years. Vareniki is another example of this. Some claim it was from Ukraine and some from Poland, but it certainly was not Russian originally.

Changes made to agriculture and food production methods directly affected what Russians were consuming. Canned foods and smoked meats were the convenience foods of a nation who lived mostly in cities and worked in offices and factories. Game meats and mushroom dishes became increasingly uncommon as people moved away from farms and into cities.

The majority of Soviet Russians were now eating meals out in canteen restaurants, which was the period's equivalent to fast food. Meals were inexpensive and served quickly. Food was prepared in bulk and dished out in the style of a cafeteria. Menu choices were quite limited and plain in taste, but most Russians had grown up with simple foods and little variety, so this wasn't a problem. Canteens were operated by the Soviet government and recipes were strictly controlled in the same way as any modern fast food franchise. A new recipe would take up to two years to be approved, and could not include any exotic or imported ingredients. Everything was geared toward mass market appeal, so there were no spices allowed since most Russians prefered bland food. The lowest common denominator dictated what was on the menu. The definition of an "outstanding chef" was one who could follow these state dictated recipes to the letter, just as chain restaurants these days have a hierarchy of management to ensure that the corporation's recipes are precisely followed.

This period also marked a shift in the primary source of protein in the Russian diet. For centuries fish had been a staple food. People had been eating local fish regularly, often being fish that someone in their family had personally caught. Now the bulk of the population moved to inner cities that were far from the source of fish. Grocery stores sold frozen fish that were often spoiled due to poor refrigeration during transport and storage. Canteens were also using frozen fish, and notorious for cooking with old and rancid oil. Fish soon acquired a bad reputation as something that tasted terrible and might even make you sick. Then, to make matters worse, numerous rivers and streams for fishing were wiped out accidentally by a series of hydraulic dam experiments that went horribly wrong. As if that wasn't bad enough, the unregulated industrial dumping of factory waste poisoned many bodies of water and destroyed entire habitats. Many of the species of fish that had been used in Russian recipes for centuries were gone forever. For all of these reasons Russians began to eat more meat than fish for the first time in their history. Because there had been so few Russian recipes for meat, new recipes were borrowed from Europe and Central Asia. This is when Shashlik started to become popular.

Another fundamental shift in diet was brought about by a change of cooking technology. City dwellings were equipped with hotplate burners that were incapable of cooking the ancient Russian clay pot recipes that roasted in a brick furnace for hours. On the other hand, this did enable Russians to fry foods. Although the technique of frying had been learned from the Tartars in the previous century, it did not become popular until the Soviet era when this equipment was in every home.

Throughout the 1930's, a trend toward healthier steamed and boiled foods was introduced by the Jewish community. This was a short lived movement though, since shortages during the second World War had Russians once again eating whatever was available. Few were particularly concerned about the long term health benefits of boiled foods when they were busy trying to survive to the next day. After shortages experienced during the two world wars, and a decade in which plain boiled foods had been popularized, Russians were again conditioned to think of eating as a means of survival, rather than something you actually enjoy.

The 1950's through 1970's were a time of renewed interest in cuisine. Many cookbooks were published in the 1960's, but they were mostly for show since they called for imported ingredients that were unobtainable. Russians would look through these books, trying to imagine what such food might taste like. Even though they couldn't make the exact recipe, they would try to imitate it with the ingredients they had available. Canteens were still serving up bland and simple foods, but Russians who had the time and money could finally experiment some with food using the information in these cookbooks.

As difficult as it is for us to imagine, it was not until the 1970's that there were finally poultry farms, and both chickens and eggs became popular for the first time. Before this time the meat was almost entirely beef, pork and lamb.

A better economy and a renewed interest in cuisine led to an appreciation of wines, particularly those from Georgia and

Moldavia. These regions have been producing international award-winning wines for centuries, but they are not widely exported to the West. This was an era when fine dining restaurants thrived in Soviet Russia, to the surprise of most people today. The best restaurants were so busy that patrons would stand outside waving money in hopes of bribing the doorman to let them get on the waiting list for a table. Meals were on a par with Western European restaurants, and the *French 75* was the cocktail of choice at the end of a meal.

Under the Soviet government, every Russian family was given a home as well as a dacha, or summer house. Dachas were a plot of land somewhere outside of the city on which owners could construct any sort of dwelling they liked with little or no regulation about building codes. Depending on one's wealth and interest in developing their dacha property, these ranged from little more than glorified toolsheds all the way up to multi-story semi-mansions. Nearly all had summer gardens where Russians would grow some of their own fruits and vegetables. This tradition continues to this day.

Things began to deteriorate in the 1980's. Shortages became so prevalent that the canteen restaurants could no longer follow the state mandated recipes, and were forced to substitute ingredients. When Soviet Russia was finally dismantled, things went from bad to worse. The deregulation of prices and collapse of the currency created a nightmare for the general population. Imagine going in to a grocery store and seeing that it cost two days of wages to buy a single loaf of bread! There was panic and widespread suffering. This went on for years, with the only relief being the food that people could grow on their own small dacha plots of land in summer, then salting and pickling everything they could to try and last through the winter. Advancement of the art of Russian cuisine had once again been trampled by economic blight.

The economy gradually improved, but it was not until well after the year 2000 that a significant number of Russians had the money to buy imported ingredients and could begin to appreciate fine dining as an enjoyable activity.

7. 21st Century Russian Cuisine (2001 to Today)

The first decade of the 21st century marked a phenomenal transformation in Russian cuisine. The accelerating availability of imported foods and seasonings provided a means by which European style restaurants could flourish. The improved economy meant more Russians were eating out and experiencing cosmopolitan cuisine. In turn, this began to gradually influence the way in which other dishes were prepared. This is very much a cuisine in flux. There is no simple definition as to what modern Russian cuisine is. It is strongly divided by economic status, age, and region. For instance, restaurants in Moscow have largely focused on presenting authentic cuisine from other parts of the world, particularly France and Japan.

Russian chef Anatoly Komm rose to meteoric fame in Russia by practicing techniques of molecular gastronomy after studying at Ferrn Adrias' famed restaurant El Bulli. Komm makes classic Russian dishes using cutting edge techniques, but such fare is

> "The problem is that for 70 years the Communist regime instilled in Russians the idea that to eat well is bad—that it is bourgeois," said Komm, expressing his frustration. *"The real problem is that in the heart of most Russians, it is enough for them to live on bread and a potato."*

unlikely to ever find its way on to the average Russian's dinner table. It is extravagant art, but it has no place in the culture.

Perhaps because Saint Petersburg does not have quite the same availability of ingredients as Moscow, and is a distant second in economic strength, one finds more down to earth changes. The city has been a melting pot of cultures ever since the time of Peter the Great. Here some of the most interesting and unique fusion dishes have been created, though many less than successfully, and often only for a flickering period at a time as chefs come and go, and restaurants open and close—sometimes in a span of just a few months. As precarious as the restaurant business is in most parts of the world, it may well be the most difficult of all to maintain in Russia.

As is inevitably the case with any new emerging style of art, or cuisine, the adherents fall under a bell curve. At one end in the smallest minority there are those who embrace everything new and different. On the other end of the spectrum are those who adamantly cling to tradition. In the center of this curve we find the majority of the population. In the case, most Russians have not yet developed a taste for concentrated flavors, or strong spices. In time this will improve, providing that the economy does not collapse again and imported ingredients remain available, even if that means you have to search for them.

Exterior of the only permanent Indian spice store in St. Petersburg. Most shops with this sort of merchandise are fly by night operations running out of the basements of buildings on a temporary basis.

Russian Recipes

Russia is a bizarre anomaly in the world: A gigantic nation without a culinary identity. Virtually all Russian cuisine falls into one of two categories. Either it was copied from another country, or it is something so simple that no recipe was ever involved, such as boiling vegetables. That isn't to say that the Russian version of things like Borscht are exactly the same as they are prepared in the country that they originated from, but they are similar enough that there is no doubt that they were copied.

The historical tapestry of reasons for this situation were explained in detail in the previous chapter. What I have provided here are a few worthwhile ancient recipes that are rarely seen outside of Russia. Of course there are many recipes for Borscht, but this specific method and balance of ingredients is something you only find in a high caliber restaurant in Russia—and Russians are very particular about their Borscht in the same way that the French are particular about Bouillabaisse.

The other recipes here are ones that you are unlikely to ever encounter anywhere, having been cobbled together from very old Russian language books published prior to the Soviet era.

POTAGE OF ROASTED LAMB AND KASHA

Kasha is defined in Eastern European cuisine as any cooked grain, most frequently buckwheat, barley or oats. Often served thin, as a kind of soup. This version is more like the type prepared in northern France that, according to legend, was introduced to the Russian aristocracy by a visiting chef around 1700. This is based on the list of ingredients used and my own experience, as the actual original recipe was probably never published and long since lost.

INGREDIENTS

600ml (21 oz)	Milk, whole
50g (1.75 oz)	Oatmeal (not instant or parboiled)
200g (7 oz)	Lamb, ground (see text below)
120g (4 oz)	Onion
30g (1 oz)	Butter
1 T	Garlic, crushed
90g (3 oz)	Peas, fresh or frozen
sprigs	Mint, fresh (optional garnish)

ADDITIONAL TIPS

For optimum and authentic results, grind your own lamb from lower leg meat. Note that lamb leg normally means the upper leg portion, but several Russian dishes prefer the so-called shin meat. If you have scraps of roasted lamb, you can use them here instead if you have a meat grinder.

PROCEDURE

1. Stir together the oatmeal and milk plus 3/4 teaspoon of salt in a braising dish with a lid. Be sure to use a large pot, since you will be adding more to it later. Put into the oven at 150°C (300°F) for 1 1/2 hours.

2A. During this time, fry the ground lamb on a HIGH heat without stirring much so as to brown well on one side before turning. After the lamb starts to brown, add the crushed garlic and remove from the heat.

2B. Alternatively, if you have roasted lamb that you will be using instead of the ground lamb, then pass it through a meat grinder. Lightly sauté the garlic in a little oil and mix it in with the ground roasted lamb.

3. When the 1 1/2 hours of braising time is up on the oatmeal, remove it from the oven and stir in the cooked lamb and garlic. Put the cover back on and return to the oven for another 1 1/2 hours at the same temperature.

4. During this time, slice the onion in thin rings and fry gently in the butter. This is the most delicate part of the recipe. The onions will need a lot of attention to brown evenly and very well without actually burning. When they are starting to brown, begin gradually reducing the heat. This will prevent them from burning and let you take them to that extreme level of caramelization that you can never reach otherwise. If you don't have experience doing this, here is your chance to practice. You have 1 1/2 hours with nothing else to do, and onions are cheap.

5. Remove from the oven and stir in the peas. Put the cover back on and allow to stand at room temperature for about 15 minutes to cool and to allow the peas to cook. To plate, a deep bowl works nicely. Add some of the onions and a few wisps of mint cut in a chiffonade over the top.

BORSCHT

The one dish that is synonymous with Russia, but like every other "Russian" food, actually came from another country. There are many regional homestyle variations, but this is what you would get in a top restaurant in Russia. This is a good soup to make ahead of time, as it is famous for getting even better after resting in the refrigerator for two or three days.

INGREDIENTS

600g (1.3 lbs)	Beef, such as chuck roast
450g (16 oz)	Cabbage, sliced to shred
400g (14 oz)	Beets - boiled until tender & peeled
90g (3oz)	Sausage, such as Kielbasa
120g (4 oz)	Tomato Purée (pasata)
120g (4 oz)	Potato, diced
90g (3 oz)	Carrot
90g (3 oz)	Celery, or Celery Root
60g (2 oz)	Red Bell Pepper
1 T	Garlic, crushed
2	Bay Leaves
2 t	Red Wine Vinegar

Also:
1 additional whole onion and carrot
Fresh Parsley and Dill
* Knorr Beef Stock gel pack (optional - see video)
Butter, Black Pepper, Smetana (or Sour Cream)

COOKING BEETS

One of the reasons why many people don't like beets is because they are used to being served beets that taste like dirt. The reason is that it is more convenient and less messy to peel beets after they are roasted or boiled. The problem is that when you roast or boil unpeeled beets, the dirt that was on the outside (you can never scrub all of it off - don't kid yourself) gets cooked right into the beets. Some people are more naturally sensitive to this taste than others. Peel the beets *before* cooking them. Add a little red wine vinegar in with the water when you are boiling them, and finally, do this on the day *before* making the Borscht, allowing the beets to rest in the refrigerator overnight before you grate them.

BORSCHT HISTORY

It is widely believed that Borscht originated in Ukraine, where there are still very distinct regional variations. The original recipe probably didn't include beets, in fact. The name comes from "borschevik", meaning hogweed. This is a plant that is delicious if you know how to pick it and handle it, but dangerous if you don't, which is probably why it isn't in the soup these days. Beets may have been what replaced the hogweed over time, and the name just lingered on. There are many versions in Russia, but they are not as well defined as the Ukranian types. The primary two types of Russian Borscht are the homestyle (simple) version and the full blown restaurant version, which is what I have shown here.

BEEF STOCK

In practice, beef stock is made for this soup separately. When I made the video, I abbreviated this process to make it more accessible to people, without sacrificing the quality too much. For the best results, use my *Best Quality Brown Beef Stock* recipe (one of my other videos on YouTube).

PROCEDURE

See video, *Borscht.*

✦

HUNTER'S FOWL

Not to be confused with the Italian dish of the same name (better known as Chicken Cacciatore). This is completely different. Also, although I have specified chicken here, a true Russian Hunter's Fowl dish from the 19th century would be prepared with a game bird that has more flavor than chicken, and benefits from a longer braise time.

INGREDIENTS

1.4 kg (3 lb)	Chicken, whole (or pheasant or grouse)
150g (5.3 oz)	Basmati Rice
120g (4 oz)	Onion, chopped coarsely
50g (1.75 oz)	Onion, grated
1 T	Flour
120g (4 oz)	Smetana, 20% (or Sour Cream)
1 T	Coriander Seeds, whole
1/2 t	Black Peppercorns, whole
1	Bay Leaf
20g (1/2 cup)	Parsley, finely chopped
2 t	Lovage, dried and crumbled (see below)
2 t	Salt

* 2 Eggs and Breadcrumbs (optional - see Step 9 on next page)
White Pepper, freshly ground

LOVAGE LEAVES

Lovage is an herb that Russians grow themselves, but it is almost never sold in stores. It is available online, and it is a delicious and very useful herb to have. It can best be described as a sweet aromatic parsley. Why this herb has not became more universally popular is a mystery, as you will see when you first experience it.

PROCEDURE

1. Break the bird down into pieces (or have your butcher do it). Remove the skin from all parts except the wings. Discard the skin. Break the back and wings down into chunks. If chicken, pound breasts to tenderize them.

2. Brown the pieces of the back with the wings in a heavy skillet on a HIGH heat (#8 out of 10) until they are golden.

3. Add the coarsely chopped onion and continue browning, reducing the heat slightly (#7 out of 10).

4. When the chicken pieces and onion are quite brown (15 minutes), add 500ml (17.6 oz) water, deglazing the pan with the first part of the water. Now add the bay leaf, coriander seeds and peppercorns. Reduce heat to MEDIUM (#5 out of 10) and simmer until the volume is about 100ml (3.5 oz) over 20-30 minutes. Pass through a sieve. Discard solids.

5. First whisk the liquid with the flour. Now mix in the grated onion, smetana, parsley and lovage. Pour over the chicken in a braising vessel.

6. Preheat oven to 200°C (390°F), but as soon as you begin cooking, lower the temperature to 150°C (250°F). Braise for 1 1/2 - 2 hours.

7. Remove chicken pieces to a bowl and reserve. Pour the liquid from the braising dish into a sauce pan and add the rice to it. Cook on a LOW heat (#3 out of 10), leaving it covered most of the time, until the rice has absorbed all of the liquid and cooked through. Taste for adequate salt.

8. This dish benefits from being refrigerated overnight and reheated the next day. When ready to serve, reheat the chicken in the oven - and ideally in a wood burning oven to give it a smokey character, or off the side on a charcoal grill outdoors. Add freshly ground white pepper.

9. Either serve with the rice, *or* create a kind of Arancini by mixing the cold rice with 1 whole egg plus 1 egg yolk. Mix to combine well. Form into balls about half the size of golf balls and roll in breadcrumbs. Deep fry until golden brown.

PORCINI AND ROASTED RYE SOUP

Deprived of spices and with a limited range of ingredients, people find ways of introducing flavors into foods that are technique driven. Based on a 17th century Russian recipe. I urge everyone who likes mushroom soup to try this for a completely unique and unexpected taste experience.

INGREDIENTS

500ml (17.6 oz)	Chicken Stock or water (see notes)
180g (6.3 oz)	Porcini or other wild mushrooms
60g (2 oz)	Roasted Rye Flour (see notes below)
75g (2.5 oz)	Smetana 20% (or sour cream)
30g (1 oz)	Butter
30g (1 oz)	Onion, grated
2-3 cloves	Garlic, crushed or minced
2 t	Salt
1/4 t	Black Pepper, finely ground

Fresh Parsley, Dill and Scallion
Additional butter for frying mushrooms

ROASTED RYE FLOUR

Preheat oven to 200°C (390°F). Spread rye flour (at least twice the amount you will actually need - it loses weight on drying) on a ceramic baking dish. Do not use metal. Roast in the oven for 15 minutes, then remove it and stir. Return to the oven for another 10-15 minutes. Surplus can be sealed in an airtight container and stored, if desired.

ADDITIONAL TIPS

Traditionally water would be used to make this, but obviously chicken stock (or vegetable stock) will bring more flavor to the dish. The taste will be bitter at first after adding the stock (or water), but the bitterness will fade during simmering. This reheats 1-3 days later especially well.

PROCEDURE

1. Clean and slice the mushrooms. Fry in butter until soft, then set aside. Add a little salt and pepper while cooking them. Note that this can be done months ahead of time when mushrooms are in season, and then kept frozen until needed.

2. On a LOW HEAT (#3 out of 10) melt the butter, then add the grated onion, crushed garlic and the salt. Fry gently for 5-7 minutes.

3. Add the toasted rye flour to the pan and stir well. You will obtain a dry crumbly mixture. Now increase the heat slightly (#4 out of 10) and roast the mixture for about 10 minutes, stirring often.

4. Add the smetana (or sour cream) and stir rapidly to form a dough that gathers into a ball. Break up the dough, then stir to recombine it. Repeat this process for 3-4 minutes to thoroughly cook the mass.

5. Add 500ml (17.6 oz) water, the black pepper and the mushrooms. Bring to a slow simmer, then cover. Maintain the simmer for 1 hour. Stir occasionally, scraping the bottom to make sure that it is not sticking and burning. Add additional water a little at a time to maintain the consistency, as needed.

6. Serve with a mixture of freshly minced parsely, dill and scallions on top. Offer additional smetana (or sour cream) on the side.

I will include more interesting and ancient
Russian recipes in Volume 2.

Cooking in Russia

YouTube Channel

Before starting this channel on YouTube, I spent a considerable time surveying the existing content by others. Nearly every video that I saw fell sharply into one of four categories. Namely:

1. Amateur home cooks giving amateur advice

2. Cooks at mediocre restaurants who are using prepackaged products for high-volume, low-quality dishes

3. Celebrity chefs who have been directed to show only the simplest dishes that can be made quickly

4. A few genuinely skilled chefs showing off their abilities, but without enough detailed information to actually reproduce key steps in what they are doing, and often requiring ingredients and skills that are outside of the bounds of even a serious home cook. Viewers writing in questions to try and get more information rarely received any reply.

I sought to address all of these problems. First, I do not give advice in aspects of cooking that I am not well versed in. I'm not going to show you how to bake wedding cakes, because I'm not a baker. I would not be offering you the best advice possible, so I will leave that to those who are experts. I only wish that others would adopt this same attitude!

Second, I don't base any dish on prepackaged products. Although occasionally an ingredient like ketchup is included, it is never the basis of a recipe.

Third, I have no directors or producers telling me that I have to make simple dishes that can be finished in 30 minutes. Most serious cooking takes time.

Finally, I try to ensure that every dish that I present is something that a serious amateur can prepare to a similar standard. I avoid elaborate plating methods on my channel, because they are intimidating and usually impractical at home. They work fine in a restaurant where you are making hundreds of the same dish every day and can order delivery of fresh microgreens by the kilogram to hand pick through for perfect and identical sprigs to garnish plates with, but that's the sort of thing that makes you dine out. It is not practical at home, nor is it necessary.

I also answer questions every day, and usually within a few hours. I do suggest that people read through the existing comments on a video before posting a question, because there is a good chance that it has already been answered if you look.

Putting videos up on YouTube inevitably draws criticism from a small percentage of viewers, and it is usually in the form of a complaint about a recipe not being sufficiently "authentic" or traditional. I have gone into some additional details about this on the first two recipes that follow on the pages ahead (*Tomato Sauce* and *Pizza Sauce*). I want to point out that there is an important difference between respecting traditions and being hamstrung by them. Just because pasta dough was always kneaded by hand using the well method, is not a reason to complain about using a food processor. You can be sure that if the Romans had electric food processors and stick blenders 1500 years ago, they would have been using them!

The Future

I will continue to post new videos on a regular basis, especially in summer when I have more available time. You are welcome to request a video on any recipe or cooking related topic. Some of my most popular videos are ones that I did at someone's request. Either leave feedback on a video, or send a private message through YouTube.

As implied on the title page of this book, this is intended only as the first volume in an annual series. I will be working on the next volume throughout 2015 and release it near the end of the year. Naturally I won't duplicate the Shopping List appendix at the back of this book again, and instead focus on new topics.

Among those topics that I will be covering in the next book are some common Russian and Georgian ingredients that are either virtually unknown or seldom used elsewhere. Those include kvas, unfiltered sunflower oil, black radishes, Khmeli suneli, red and green sour plums (as Tkemali), lovage, and dill. While dill is well known, it is much more versatile than people realize. I've considered writing an entire book on nothing but dill recipes, in fact.

Thank you for all of your support, and I hope we can continue to make this channel a success by sharing it with your friends and family in the years ahead!

TOMATO SAUCE

If I had to pick the single most important preparation in any modern kitchen, tomato sauce would be it. Why? Because it is used in so many recipes and no commercially made product comes even remotely close to what you can make yourself.

INGREDIENTS

75 ml (2 1/2 oz)	Extra Virgin Olive Oil (in all)
30 g (1 oz)	Butter
5-6 cloves	Garlic, crushed with the side of a knife
300g (10 oz)	Puréed Tomatoes (boxed Italian Pasata)
1 t	Brown Sugar
45g (1 1/2 oz)	Onion, diced
120g (4 oz)	Cherry Tomatoes, quartered
1/2 t	Black Pepper, medium fine ground
1 t	Lemon Zest (freshly grated)
30 ml (1 oz)	Red Wine, dry
30 ml (1 oz)	White Wine, dry
30 ml (1 oz)	Vodka
1/4 t	Cayenne Pepper
1 T	Basil, freshly minced
	or substitute 1 t Knorr Basil paste
10 ml (2 t)	Red Wine Vinegar (best quality)

ADDITIONAL TIPS

Do not attempt to scale up this recipe by any significant amount if you are using a home stove. I explain this in the introduction of this book. This is very much a restaurant method. It is a quick way to produce an excellent product. If you plan to simmer this for hours in the traditional way, then you don't need to cook the garlic in butter first and your caramelization at the start will not be quite as important if you don't do a perfect job of it.

COMPLAINTS DEPARTMENT

Vodka is a well established ingredient in Italian restaurant kitchens for making tomato sauces, though rare in Italian home kitchens. The difference between home and restaurant cooking is more than most people realize. Alcohol extracts flavors from tomatoes that are not water soluble. No, you can not leave out the wine and obtain good results. Consider that the amount of alcohol naturally present in ripe fruit is more than in a sauce cooked with a modest amount of spirits! If you eat ripe fruit and give fruit to your children, then there is no reason to fear alcohol in cooking.

PROCEDURE

1. Gently fry the whole garlic cloves in a mixture of the butter with a tablespoon of the olive oil. Set aside.

2. Heat a second heavy-bottom, non-reactive pan. When it is hot, add the rest of the olive oil. Wait for the oil to just start smoking.

3. Add half of the puréed tomatoes (pasata). Beware of splattering!

4. Do not stir. Add the sugar and salt. Wait without stirring.

5. When the bubbles get smaller, add the onion and cherry tomatoes. Now you can stir. Fold the mixture together and lower the heat.

6. When the tomatoes have mostly melted into the sauce, add the rest of the pasata (tomato purée) plus the lemon zest, black pepper and the previously cooked brown butter-garlic.

7. Stir until hot again. Add the red and white wine with the vodka. Stir and partially cover. Cook for 10 minutes on medium heat.

8. Add the cayenne pepper and stir. Make sure nothing is sticking to the bottom of the pan. Partially cover again for another 5 minutes.

9. Add the basil and move off the heat. Cool briefly before using a stick blender to homogenize. Add the red wine vinegar during the blending.

PIZZA SAUCE

Closely related to the previous Tomato Sauce recipe, this is your secret weapon for producing quality pizzas at home.

INGREDIENTS

60ml (2 oz)	Olive Oil
500g (17.5 oz)	Puréed Tomatoes (boxed Italian Pasata)
180g (6 oz)	Tomatoes, cored and diced coarsely
2 t	Sugar
1 t	Italian Paprika Forte (see note below)
120g (4 oz)	Onion, diced
1 t	Oregano, dried
1 t	Basil, dried
1 t	Black Pepper, coarsely ground
* 1 t	MSG (optional)
6-8 cloves	Garlic
30g (1 oz)	Parmigiano-Reggiano, grated fine
60ml (2 oz)	Red Wine Vinegar
30 ml (1 oz)	White Wine, dry

ADDITIONAL TIPS

By "hot paprika", I am referring to Italian *Paprika Forte*. You can use any paprika, but this type will produce the best result. Do not substitute cayenne.

This is one of the very few times that I call for dried basil, but this is strictly for reasons of economy. You may use fresh, but because of the high heat and other strong flavors, it won't make much difference. Replacing the dried oregano and basil with a couple of tablespoons of fresh herbs will improve this sauce a bit, but in restaurants we don't, because dried herbs are inexpensive and most customers won't appreciate the difference.

56

COMPLAINTS DEPARTMENT

This recipe has received criticism for being too potent, but this is intentional because a pizza should have a thin layer of sauce applied with a brush. If you ladle it on, the way that many pizzerias do, then this will indeed be overwhelming—but applied in moderation, this will produce a result that no one will complain about. It is based on a family recipe at a pizzeria in Venice, Italy, that dates back to 1954.

PROCEDURE

1. Heat a heavy-bottom, non-reactive pan. When it is hot, add the olive oil. Wait for the oil to just start smoking.

3. Add 100g (3 oz) of the puréed tomatoes. Beware of splattering!

4. Do not stir. Add the sugar, paprika and salt.

5. After a minute it will be slightly darker. Now you can stir.

6. After 5 minutes when the oil separates from the tomato sauce, add the onion. Reduce heat and cook until the onions are soft (about 10 mins.)

7. Add the rest of the puréed tomatoes, the red wine vinegar, the oregano, the basil, the black pepper, and the MSG (if you are using it). Stir in the cubed tomatoes.

8. Partially cover and cook for 15 minutes on medium to medium-high.

9. Add the sliced garlic, parmesan cheese and white wine. Stir until the cheese is melted completely into the sauce.

10. Move off the heat and purée with a stick blender. Taste and adjust the salt level. Remember that this is not a pasta sauce. It is supposed to be very intense, so make it saltier than you would normally.

FILET MIGNON & WHISKY MARINADE

This cooking method will produce the same ultra-pro results delivered by the likes of Morton's, Smith & Wollensky, and other specialty steakhouse restaurants.

In an effort to please everyone by not offending tea-totalers and make menus "child friendly", as well as reducing costs, very few restaurants today still feature hard liquor in recipes. That's unfortunate, because some of the finest recipes from decades ago have been almost completely forgotten as a result. This is a perfect example of that.

FOR THE MARINADE

45ml (1.5 oz)	Olive Oil
* 30ml (1 oz)	Scotch Whisky (see note below)
4 cloves	Garlic
2 t (10 ml)	Worcestershire Sauce
1 t	Thyme, dried
3/4 t	Black Pepper, finely ground
3/4 t	MSG (Accent flavor enhancer)
* 1/4-1/2 t	Liquid Smoke (see note below)

---

* For a stronger Scotch flavor, use a smokey one such as those from Islay. Otherwise an excellent and economical choice is William Lawson's Scotch together along with a few drops of liquid smoke.

ADDITIONAL TIPS

Experiment with the amount of time you leave the meat in the marinade (15 minutes on up to a couple of hours). You have to find the balance that you prefer. Be sure to use warm plates for serving.

HISTORY

I must confess that of the many different types of restaurants I have worked in, or been involved with, I have never worked in a dedicated steakhouse, and I discovered this secret in an odd way. The person I was dining with requested that their steak not have any char marks on it because they believed that the char marks were where the carcinogens were at. This was a peculiar request that the restaurant apparently had not been prepared for, and they were forced to confess that all of their steaks had the char marks already on them. In fact, that searing wasn't even done at the restaurant. The meat was shipped to them from a central facility where the first stage of the cooking was done by machine. All they did is pop the steaks in the oven to finish them off. Why have a machine cooking them? More precise control at a high volume, and a product that arrives at the retail outlet virtually idiot proof. The results were very good, but this one I am showing you here is even better. The marinade is more flavorful, and using the torch on it at the end instead of the start, gives a caramelized crust that the factory method can't deliver.

PROCEDURE

See video, *PERFECT Steakhouse FILET MIGNON with Whisky Marinade.*

RIBEYE STEAK

No other piece of meat so often fails to live up to its potential as a ribeye steak. The reason is that it is so naturally tender and flavorful that many cooks imagine themselves to be experts at cooking steak, when the cut itself is the only thing that's right.

	FOR THE SPICE RUB
1 t	Cumin Seeds
1 t	Garlic Powder
1 t	Black Peppercorns
1 t	Knorr Demi Glace powder
	or a Knorr beef stock cube
1/2 t	Paprika
1/2 t	Rosemary, dried
1/2 t	Anise Seeds
2 t	Coarse Salt
2 t	Turbinado Sugar
1 t	MSG (Accent flavor enhancer)

Grind the spices together except for the salt, sugar and MSG, which should be mixed in by hand after grinding.

ADDITIONAL TIPS

Experiment using a Jaccard device, if you haven't already. Only the finest steaks do not benefit from this treatment. Get the one that has three rows of blades. The single-row unit is not nearly as effective.

SOME PERSONAL HISTORY

My very first job cooking in 1968 was grilling steaks and burgers at a small diner owned by the father of one of my friends. One day when the place was overflowing with customers and the cooks had quit after a fight with him, in a desperate state of panic, he asked me if I knew how to cook. I assured him that I did, even though I had no real experience. Flinching, and unsure of what to do, he reluctantly trusted me to tend to the stove for "just a couple of minutes", since he had to take orders and run the register. The few minutes went on for an hour. Finally when the lunch rush had slowed down, he made his way back to the kitchen. To my surprise, he wasn't telling me to stop cooking. Instead he was just standing there watching what I was doing as I finished up the last order. What happened next was a turning point in my life. He told me that several customers had said it was the best meat they had ever had, and that he knew it wasn't the meat because it all came from the same place where he always bought it. He cut a small bite out of one of the steaks I had just prepared for a customer to taste it for himself. I still vividly remember his eyes growing as big as saucers. He couldn't believe it was the same steak that he had been destroying. I was immediately hired for the rest of that summer.

The reason was that my father was friends with the owners of two of the best restaurants in San Francisco, and on more than a few occasions I was turned over to the chefs there to "train" while the other adults socialized and drank. It was not serious training, of course. They understood that the owner just wanted me entertained in some way, but the kitchens were often busy and they had to find things I could do to keep me occupied. It wasn't until I found myself manning the stove at that diner that I realized how many lessons I'd absorbed, and that this was something that I was actually capable of doing better than most adults, which is an overwhelming feeling for an 11 year old.

PROCEDURE

See video, *The PERFECT Ribeye Steak - Including Smoked Steak.*

TOURNEDOS ROSSINI

It is important to appreciate that tastes have changed since the 19th century. People eat much less fat now and are accustomed to much stronger flavors. The idea of using garlic and chili peppers back then was almost unheard of. These days if you simply fry a filet mignon up in some butter, it will be seen as bland and uninspired. This has much more flavor.

FOR THE SAUCE

250ml	Demi-glace (or strong beef or veal stock)
90g (3 oz)	Tomatoes, strained puréed pasata
60g (2 oz)	Shallots
30g (1 oz)	Garlic cloves
1/2	Red Chili, seeded and scraped
60g (2 oz)	Butter
250ml (1 cup)	Red Wine, dry (divided in portions)
1 t	Sherry Vinegar
1-2 t	Fresh Herbs, minced

* If you love spicy food and find yourself tempted to increase the amount of red chili here, my advice is to try it the original way first.

FOR THE ONION JAM

150g (5 oz)	Onions
1 T	Sugar
90ml (3 oz)	Beef Stock, or Veal Stock
30ml (1 oz)	Madeira, or good sherry
2 t	Parsley, freshly chopped

ADDITIONAL TIPS

In lieu of the foie gras, you can substitute a slice of pâté, but be sure that it is excellent quality. Cheap pâté has an offensive after taste that will ruin this dish. If you are really in a pinch, you can add a few drops of quality Italian or French truffle oil to some minced black olives to top this with in place of the slice of truffle. This works surprisingly well.

OTHER INGREDIENTS

Beef (see video)
Bacon
Foie Gras, or Pâté (see video)
Black Truffle slices (or substitute as explained below)
Chanterelles (for plating)
Tomato (for platng)

NOTES

The original classic version of this dish is extremely basic in terms of cooking technique. The only serious skill required is in making the sauce perfectly silky, like you see in the photo in this video. The old school method (which I used) is to use a carefully prepared, well-skimmed demi-glace and pass the sauce through a very fine sieve multiple times. The modern restaurant way of doing this is with a device called a Thermomix, which can make almost anything perfectly smooth, but the machine is prohibitively expensive for households, costing thousands of dollars.

PROCEDURE

See video, *TOURNEDOS ROSSINI.*

MEDIEVAL PORK ON TRENCHERS

This is obviously the ancestor of Osso Buco, but it is faster to prepare and a time-tested favorite of every meat lover.

INGREDIENTS

2	Pork Neck steaks, cut very thick
45g (1.5 oz)	Shallot, brunois
45g (1.5 oz)	Carrot, brunois
45g (1.5 oz)	Celery, brunois
2-4	Garlic cloves
1	Bay Leaf
sprigs	Thyme, fresh
90ml (3 oz)	White Wine, dry
60ml (2 oz)	Demi-glace (or stock)
2 slices	Bread, thick

ADDITIONAL TIPS

Do not attempt to make this with lean pork. It will be dry and stringy. Pork neck is something you may have to ask your butcher for, depending on what country you are in. You want well marbled pork. I suggest using sourdough bread. If you love garlic, this dish is especially well suited to adding much more garlic than the basic recipe given here. Indulge yourself and serve the pan-roasted cloves along with the meat.

NOTES

Medieval cooking would only include a slab of meat like this for nobility. Most people could not afford much meat, and about a third of the year people were barred from eating any meat due to various religious observances. This dish is really at its best if you can obtain wild boar neck, but then you will need to braise it for even longer. The flavor of boar compared to a farmed pig is reminiscent of the difference between wine and grape juice. The latter goes down easier, but the former is far more intense and interesting.

WINE NOTES

My choice for this dish is an Valpolicella Ripasso, sometimes labeled as an Amarone Ripasso. This is an Italian wine produced by passing aged Valpolicella through the pomace of Amarone. The resulting wine has more tannin, a darker color, more alcohol and a more concentrated flavor. It is also available at a reasonable price, as quality wines go. This is one of the great hidden treasures often overlooked because it is not well known.

Cesari and Bussola are excellent examples of this style of winemaking, but these specific choices may be difficult to find, so ask your local wine merchant what would be similar.

PROCEDURE

See video, *MEDIEVAL ROAST PORK ON TRENCHERS.*

ULTIMATE CLASSIC BURGER

There are three families of burgers: the prime steakhouse burger made only from premium cuts, the frozen patty that contains a careful blend of meats, and what most home cooks make, which is store-bought ground beef. The latter is the easiest, but also the least flavorful by a large margin.

FOR THE GROUND BEEF

600g (1.3 lbs)	Beef (see Additional Tips below)
100g (3 1/2 oz)	Beef or Veal Liver
80g (3 oz)	Butter
1 t	Coarse Salt
1/2 t	MSG (optional)

ADDITIONAL TIPS

Beef shank adds a deep rich flavor, but ideally you will also grind in trim from tenderloin and a bit of sirloin, too. The exact balance is a matter of personal taste, so you should experiment with different ratios to see what you prefer. The ratio of 6 parts of beef to 1 part of liver is unlikely to be improved on, no matter what cuts of beef you are using. Try grinding in a little bacon, but don't go overboard. Keep it subtle.

When making up your burger, the mistake that most home cooks make is not using enough dressing compared to what a restaurant uses, and not using very-finely sliced onion. Use a mandoline to cut your onions super thin.

HISTORY

For a couple of years my mother worked for a high caliber meat company with their own ranch. They sold primarily to independent butcher shops back in the day when such places were found on every major street in every city, and supermarkets were for the less discriminating. They decided to expand their business into restaurants, but now they were faced with how to divide the less desirable cuts so as not to waste meat. What we saw was pretty much common sense. The nastiest pieces were ground up with just enough "real meat" to hold the sinew, fat and membranes together. The biggest customers for this bargain basement meat was a conglomerate of bowling alleys and a group of drive-in movie theaters that offered grilled burgers at their snack bar. You've probably had this sort of burger before. It tends to leave a lasting impression.

Then there were the high-end steakhouses that wanted to offer a burger that was as mouth-watering and flavorful as their steaks. For a while the meat company was giving my mother samples of all of their different attempts to craft the optimum burger for us to try at home and give them detailed feedback. We cooked some on the stove, some in the broiler and some on an outdoor BBQ pit. What we found was quite surprising. The best taste came from thin burgers that went straight from the freezer to the grill. The reason is because they had liver in them, and liver contains active enzymes that react with the meat they are in the presence of. Because they were thin, they would defrost and cook in a single step, and because they had been frozen, the enzymes had not had time to react with the meat. If you wanted a bigger burger, you just cook more patties and put them together, the way that most hamburger places do. So, my advice is to make these up as thin patties and freeze them. Cook them straight out of the freezer on a BBQ for maximum enjoyment.

PROCEDURE

See video, *Ultimate Classic BURGER*

PORK CHOPS IN ALE

The combination of beer and pork always looks good on paper, but in practice most recipes produce very disappointing results. It is all about the delicate balance. This yields a deep rich brown aromatic glaze that isn't the least bit bitter.

FOR THE MARINADE	
1 t	Brown Mustard Seeds
3/4 t	Caraway Seeds
1/2 t	Black Peppercorns
1/4 t	Coriander Seeds
1 1/2 t	Brown Sugar, preferably Cassonade
6 cloves	Garlic
* 1/2	Red Chili, seeded
45ml (1.5 oz)	Vegetable Oil
30ml (1 oz)	Dill Pickle Juice (from jar)
1 t	Salt

* If you love spicy food and find yourself tempted to increase the amount of red chili here, my advice is to try it the original way first.

OTHER INGREDIENTS	
800g (1.75 lbs)	Pork Chops, not too lean
120g (4 oz)	Onion, coarsely chopped
180ml (6.5 oz)	Newcastle Brown Ale
	or substitute Baltika #4 Russian beer
15g (1/2 oz)	Onion, finely chopped
1 T	Sage or Dill, minced
2 t	Mustard Oil (see video)
	Black Pepper, fresh ground

ADDITIONAL TIPS

Experiment with adding the onions much later than you see in the video. If you add them early on (as shown), you get a very onion-flavored sauce. If you add them later, you still get a rich brown sauce, but visible pieces of onion. Both are good, but different. It is important to use good quality marbled pork for this, such as Berkshire. You can also make this using pork neck, but the sauce will be rather greasy, which many people object to these days.

HISTORY

Early on in my career cooking, I tried many times to develop a good recipe for this seemingly natural pairing of pork and beer, but no matter what I tried, I didn't like the end result. Bitterness, metallic tastes, and synthetic notes plagued every attempt. I stopped trying until I encountered a street vendor in Amsterdam who sold pork cooked in Belgian ales. He was dedicated to the idea of cooking with ale (as are many Belgian chefs, by the way), and the experience rekindled my desire to find a way to make this dish work. I'm happy to say that this recipe is every bit as good as his, and perhaps even better.

PROCEDURE

See video, *Pork Chops in Newcastle Brown Ale.*

SMOKED BABY BACK PORK RIBS

These are the sort of ribs that you can win contests with. They are better tasting than almost any rib joint you can find. One reason is the wine used to cook them in, which is an expensive ingredient that rib places don't use because customers won't pay that much money for a plate of ribs, no matter how good they taste. So right off the bat you have an advantage over restaurants that are operated for profit.

FOR THE RIBS

1.4kg (3 lbs)	Pork Baby Back Ribs
1 t	Black Peppercorns
1 t	Cumin
1 t	Paprika
1 t	Smoked Paprika (Pimentón)
1/2 t	Ajwain
	or substitute 1 t Thyme
1 T	Dark Brown Sugar (Muscovado)
2 t	Coarse Salt
500ml (2 cups)	Red Wine (see notes below)
90g (3 oz)	Carrot
90g (3 oz)	Onion
1 head	Garlic
1-2	Chili Peppers, red

ADDITIONAL TIPS

The type of wine you use here will play an important role in the final dish. Not only because the ribs are getting flavor from it, but also remember that ultimately it is in the sauce at the end. You can use a moderately priced red wine from Chile with good results, but if you want spectacular contest-winning results, up your investment to a high-alcohol content Zinfandel from Napa. Although wine enthusiasts may disagree with my simplified rule here, but the fact is that it works - there is a nearly linear relationship between the alcohol content of a Zinfandel and the potency of its flavor profile. For best results, find a wine that is at least 14.5% alcohol. The most stunning, mind-bending Zinfandel comes from Martinelli's vineyards with some vintages being nearly 18% alcohol. It is something you have to taste to believe. But that is excessive. You don't need *that* level of refinement for this. Unless money is no object.

FOR THE SAUCE

Pork stock	All of it from cooking the ribs, defatted
100g (3.5 oz)	Ketchup
100g (3.5 oz)	Sugar
50g (1.75 oz)	Apple Cider Vinegar
50g (1.75 oz)	Red Wine Vinegar
1 t	Mustard, prepared
1 t	Liquid Smoke, preferably mesquite

HISTORY

Like most other barbecue enthusiasts, I used to believe that the only way to do things was slow smoking, and that boiling or pressure cooking ribs was heresy. Then I met Tony Roma. He used to hang out in the Beverly Hills location of his restaurant chain almost every night for many years. In case you don't know, Roma's ribs have won countless contests and first place awards just about everywhere they have been entered. He pressure cooks them. Personally, I don't even like the type of rib that has been cooked entirely by smoking any more. It tastes carcinogenic because it is. But, to each their own. Try this and you won't be disappointed. I promise you.

PROCEDURE

See video, *Smoked Baby Back Pork Ribs with BBQ Sauce* .

FRENCH CHICKEN WITH LENTILS

This lengthy recipe shows the complete preparation of both the chicken quarters and the roulade made from the breasts.

INGREDIENTS

1.5kg (3.25 lb)	Chicken, whole
500ml (2 cups)	Red Wine, dry
30ml (1 oz)	Cognac
2 t	Sherry Vinegar
1/2	Knorr Chicken Stock Cube
	or 200ml chicken stock (see video)
500ml (2 cups)	Veal Stock
15ml (1/2 oz)	Lemon Juice, fresh
30g (1 oz)	Butter
1 egg yolk	

Bay Leaves, Juniper Berries, Black Peppercorns
Onions, Celery, Carrots, Garlic
Fresh Thyme and Tarragon
Mushrooms, preferably wild

ADDITIONAL TIPS

Be sure to use a quality free range chicken, and preferably a young or a small heritage variety. These will be much more flavorful and will turn this dish into something spectacular. The problem with heritage variety chickens is that they can be tough if you are not using a recipe that is suited to them. This recipe is perfectly suited.

Also, what should be stressed is the need to deeply caramelize the chicken carcass to make the sauce from. If you don't really brown it, you won't have the depth of flavor that this dish depends on.

HISTORY

As I remarked in the video, this recipe came from an appearance by Marco Pierre White in the seventh season of the Australian MasterChef television series. I saw this as a classic case of how the misconception of how restaurant food is prepared is unwittingly passed on to people. The average customer imagines that when they place an order for something that takes hours to make, that the restaurant kitchen must be like some kind of conveyer belt with each dish having been started hours earlier on the chance that a customer might wander in and want it, so that it can be delivered to their table fresh and hot. Virtually no restaurant operates that way. First, because the amount of food wasted would be staggering. Second, because if suddenly ten orders for a particular dish arrived, the kitchen would still be in the same boat, unable to deliver the order until everything had been made from scratch. Aside from simple things like steaks and burgers, most of what you are getting in a restaurant is largely reheated food that was made anywhere from earlier that day to several weeks ago, depending on the item and the standards of that particular establishment.

PROCEDURE

See video, *Classic French Chicken with Lentils.*

BLOWTORCH CHICKEN

This is really a very simple recipe when you get right down to it, but it doesn't give that impression when it is served up with flame-crisped bubbling golden skin.

INGREDIENTS

1.6kg (3.5 lbs)	Chicken, whole
120ml (4oz)	Orange Juice
1 T	Orange Zest
60g (2 oz)	Onions, chopped
2-4	Red Serrano Chilies, fresh (used 2 places)
1-2	Dried Chilies (your choice)
90g (3 oz)	Sugar
3-4	Garlic cloves, coarsely chopped
60g (2 oz)	Butter
1 T	Lime or Lemon Juice, fresh
1/2 t	Tabasco Chipotle Sauce (optional)
30ml (1 oz)	White Balsamic Vinegar
	* or substitute Rice Wine Vinegar
2 T	Scallions, minced

ADDITIONAL TIPS

If you are cooking this in the oven, put the chicken on a wire rack. Initially put it breast-side down, and then flip it over about 3/4 of the way through the cooking time. This will keep the skin crisp on all sides. Better still is to cook it on a grill outdoors, but that's not always possible. Use two blowtorches simultaneously at the table if you have them.

For even more drama, warm some rum up, set it on fire, and pour it over the chicken just before you bring it out to the table so that it is a ball of fire. Just be careful not to ignite yourself in the process.

COCKTAILS AND FOOD

If I had to pick a single cuisine that is my favorite, it is pseudo-Polynesian food such as this. Probably because of growing up in the shadow of Trader Vic, as I explained in detail in my cocktail book. However, beyond that, the combination of cocktails with food that is sweet, sour, salty and spicy, is the most extreme taste sensation humanly possible to achieve. You are stimulating all of your taste senses at once, and the alcohol helps carry flavor molecules into your olfactory glands as vapors. If you are drinking a non-alcoholic beverage, you will never get the full taste sensation that a dish like this one offers.

PROCEDURE

See video, *BLOWTORCH CHICKEN.*

STUFFED MUSHROOMS

For over a century, these have been one of the most universally popular appetizers at parties. It wasn't until the poor quality frozen ready-made stuffed mushrooms invaded supermarkets that they fell out of favor with the general public. Homemade stuffed mushrooms are every bit as delicious now as they were decades ago.

INGREDIENTS

8	Large Mushrooms
1/2	Lemon (for juice)
45g (1.5 oz)	Bacon
60g (2oz)	Red Onion, diced
22g (3/4 oz)	Garlic, chopped coarsely
60g (2 oz)	Shrimp, shelled
1/2 t	Paprika
30ml (1 oz)	White Wine, dry
2	Egg Yolks
2 T	Bread Crumbs

Cayenne to taste (from a pinch to 1/2 teaspoon)
Parmesan Cheese (for grating - see video)

ADDITIONAL TIPS

Excellent results are also obtained by substituting crab, mussels, clams, or even oysters for the shrimp. In the case of crab, I suggest also substituting sherry for the white wine. In the case of oysters, stay with the white wine, but add finely ground black pepper and a little ketchup. I realize that this is a lot of work for only eight mushrooms, so I advise you to scale it up accordingly to make it worth your time. Remember that once you get them prepared, you can store them and finish them up later on demand.

HISTORY

In the suburbs of San Francisco where I grew up, stuffed mushrooms were the ubiquitous appetizer at every social event, ranging from high school dances and church fund raisers to wedding anniversaries and family holiday gatherings. Apart from the time-honored tradition of running the barbecue outdoors, preparing stuffed mushrooms was one of the few culinary tasks that was socially approved for Dad to try his hand at. My theory as to why this exception was made is because it was a recipe that appeared in so many cocktail books and men's magazines in the 1950's.

Stuffed mushrooms originated in 19th century France, where the stuffing was invariably some type of sausage. This coincided with the first commercially cultivated mushrooms. Before that the only mushrooms were ones you foraged yourself. Many years later they became popular in Italy, and these days they are more often associated with Italian cuisine than French, but that's because they have remained popular in Italy and not because they were invented there. The idea of using seafood instead of sausage seems to have its origins in New York City in the early 20th century, when oysters were incredibly popular. Somewhere around that time, February 4th was declared Stuffed Mushroom Day in the United States, and some restaurants still celebrate it to this day.

PROCEDURE

See video, *Best STUFFED MUSHROOMS with Shrimp and Bacon.*

FRIED CHICKEN

Aside from being less greasy than chicken that has been cooked all the way through by deep frying, this method provides for a way to intensify the chicken flavor in the meat itself.

	SEASONING MIX
2 t	Black Peppercorns, whole
1 1/2 t	Rosemary, dried
1 t	Thyme, dried
1 t	Oregano, dried
1 t	Sage, dried
1 t	Chives, dried
1 t	Garlic Powder
3/4 t	Turmeric (or substitute Curry Powder)
3/4 t	Paprika
1/2 t	Nutmeg
1/2 t	Cayenne
2 t	Sugar
1 1/2 t	Salt
1/2 t	MSG (Accent flavor enhancer)
60g (2 oz)	Flour
2 T	Polenta (do not substitute grits or corn meal)
2 t	Baking Powder

ADDITIONAL TIPS

This is a recipe that really benefits from the freshest and best quality spices and herbs you can obtain. The turmeric and paprika help create the golden color, but don't really contribute that much flavor, so you can adjust the desired color by changing the proportion of these two spices. You can use any chicken parts you like, but if you are doing a large quantity, such as for a banquet or other restaurant application, using all one type of part will ensure that they cook in the same amount of time.

HISTORY

My next door neighbor who won State Fair fried chicken contests

using this pressure-cooked approach, but she did not deep fry the chicken parts. Instead she pan fried them in Crisco, a brand of vegetable shortening. If you want contest-winning flavor, do the same thing. Melt enough vegetable shortening to come about halfway up the chicken pieces. You can also use lard. The result with lard is perceived as "incredibly better" by some, "not much different" by others, and actually "worse" by a small minority, so experiment and see what you prefer. In a restaurant we generally deep fry for convenience, unless the guest is VIP. On the subject of lard, these days most people cringe at the idea of using it, but the fact is numerous studies have concluded that it is no more unhealthy than vegetable oil, and some claim it is actually better for you.

PROCEDURE

See video, *Best FRIED CHICKEN - American 1950 Style.*

KOREAN SWEET CRISPY CHICKEN

This is a popular street food in Korea. The same approach that was used in making the fried chicken in the previous recipe can also be applied to other dishes to make them less greasy and more tender.

<u>INGREDIENTS</u>

1-3	Dried Chilies (see video)
4	Garlic cloves
30ml (1 oz)	Soy Sauce
150ml (5 oz)	Chicken Stock
3-4 T	Honey
60ml (2 oz)	Bae Gochu Sigcho (Pear-Chili Vinegar)
	* See next page over
2 T	Potato Starch (or corn starch)
10	Chicken Wings

For plating: Scallions, Sesame Seeds, Red Chili Pepper

ADDITIONAL TIPS

The sauce can be made up in larger amounts and stored in the refrigerator for up to a week without too much loss in flavor. Make it a little spicier than you want it if you are preparing it a day or more ahead of time, since the heat diminishes on storage. As in my other recipes, I urge you to dry your own chili peppers for maximum flavor.

PROCEDURE

See video, *Spicy KOREAN SWEET CRISPY CHICKEN - Dakgangjeong.*

BAE GOCHU SIGCHO

If you can buy the authentic Bae Gochu Sigcho from Korea, do so because the commercial product is better, but this is an acceptable imitation.

BAE GOCHU SIGCHO (PEAR-CHILI VINEGAR)	
350ml (12 oz)	Apple Cider Vinegar
200g (7 oz)	Pear, fresh
15g (1/2 oz)	Red Chili Pepper
1/2 t	Salt

ADDITIONAL TIPS

Try mixing some of this with a little White Miso paste (available in Asian specialty stores) and a pinch of sugar to make a delicious Korean salad dressing.

PROCEDURE

See video, *Korean PEAR & RED CHILI VINEGAR.*

INDONESIAN FUSION POTATOES

Although in the video I presented this as a recipe for mashed potatoes, it can be made with pieces of whole potato, which is more similar to the original Indonesian dish that this recipe is based on.

SEASONING MIX

600g (1.3 lbs)	Potatoes
30g (1 oz)	Peanuts
1 T	Sesame Seeds
1 t	Coriander Seeds
5-6	Cloves, whole (the spice - not garlic)
1-2	Dried Red Chili Peppers (Serrano)
1/2 t	Turmeric
100g (3.5 oz)	Onion, sliced
100g (3.5 oz)	Tomato, coarsely diced
1	Bay Leaf
2-3 cloves	Garlic, coarsely chopped
100g (3.5 oz)	Butter (55 g first, 45g later)
1/2 t	Marjoram
2 T	Parsley, freshly minced
Mayonnaise (optional - see video)	
Fresh Ground Black Pepper	

ADDITIONAL TIPS

Try this with cubes of par-boiled potatoes for a different version of the same dish. If you like spicy food, this dish can withstand more chili peppers, and by all means dry roast your own chilies for the maximum flavor. This is a simplified western-friendly version and a bit tame. It is easy to see how this can be modified to yield very intense flavors, as are customary in authentic street foods. For a more authentic experience, swap out the butter for a mixture of chili oil and mustard oil.

HISTORY

Although most westerners regard potatoes as a side dish, in India and Southeast Asia, potatoes are often regarded as a complete meal. A very similar dish to this is a common street food in Indonesia and Singapore. While the term "street food" conjures images of fly-by-night taco trucks and hot dog venders in the minds of most Americans, there are highly reputable street food venders in Malaysia that have been family operated businesses for generations. They have survived because they have recipes and methods to produce tantalizing delicacies that are often impossible to imitate.

PROCEDURE

See video, *Mashed Potatoes - INDONESIAN STYLE Fusion Potato Curry.*

OSSOBUCO

A grand classic of Italian cuisine that is too often turned into something mediocre by a lack of attention to detail.

INGREDIENTS

900 g (2 lb)	Veal Shanks
1 T	Coarse Salt
3 T	Flour
3 T	Olive Oil
120 g (4 oz)	Onion, diced small
60 g (2 oz)	Celery, diced small
60 g (2 oz)	Carrot, diced small
80 g (2 3/4 oz)	Italian Tomato Purée (pasata)
6-8 cloves	Garlic, thinly sliced
30 ml (1 oz)	Sherry, rich Olorosso
30 ml (1 oz)	Cognac
1 T	Balsamic Vinegar (optional)
250 ml (1 cup)	Beef Stock
1 1/2 t	Rosemary, dried

Fresh Parsley, Lemon Zest and crushed Garlic for the Gremolata
Black Pepper, freshly ground

HISTORY OF OSSOBUCO AND TOMATOES

This dish is not nearly as old as most people imagine. A encyclopedic cookbook published in Italy in 1920 makes no mention of Ossobuco existing, which has led food historian Clifford Wright to believe that Ossobuco was an invention of restaurants in Lombardy some time later. The tomato itself has changed a great deal just since the mid-20th century, believe it or not. It was only about 70 years ago when a mutant tomato that was bright red was discovered. This was promptly cross bred to produce the commercial varieties that we have today. Unfortunately, that also has a rather poor flavor profile compared to the previous varieties. For more about this, Google search: "Flavor Is Price of Scarlet Hue of Tomatoes".

PROCEDURE

1. Salt and flour the meat. Heat pan on HIGH heat setting.

2. Brown the pieces very well one at a time. Take them just to the edge of being burnt, but not actually charcoal.

3. Add the mirepoix so that the liquid that comes off of the vegetables deglazes the pan. Reduce the heat to MEDIUM-HIGH. You may add a little Balsamic vinegar at this point.

4. After 3-4 minutes when the vegetables have softened some, add the tomato purée and half of the garlic.

5. After another 4-5 minutes of cooking, add the sherry wine.

6. Cook until most of the liquid has evaporated, then add the cognac.

7. Cook until mostly dry again, then add the white wine and the beef stock. Bring to a boil and simmer for 5 minutes.

8. Put a little of the sauce down in the braising vessel, then put the meat on top of it. Pour the rest of the sauce over the top, piling the cooked vegetables up on top of the meat. Put the rest of the garlic on top of the meat so that the condensate trickles down through the garlic and vegetables while it is braising. Also add the rosemary and some freshly ground coarse black pepper on top.

9. Roast at 160°C (320°F) for 1 hour, then lower the oven temperature to 130°C (265°F) for 2 more hours.

10. Strain and reduce the sauce. Prepare the gremolata and plate. Ideally serve this with Risotta alla Milanese (on the next page of this book).

RISOTTO ALLA MILANESE

The steps involved for making this risotto are basically the same for any risotto. The only complication here is the marrow.

FOR PREPARING THE MARROW

1 Marrow Bone
1 t Kosher Salt
1 T Apple Cider Vinegar
Cold water to cover

REGARDING THE MARROW

The pre-cooking of the marrow produces a cleaner taste and a silkier texture between the grains of rice. As a bonus, cooked marrow will keep for much longer without fear of spoilage, which is logistically very useful in a restaurant where it is impossible to anticipate how many orders will be placed on any given day.

INGREDIENTS

260g (9.2 oz)	Carnarolli Rice (Arborio is not as good)
2.5 Liters (3 qts)	Chicken Stock
90-120ml (3-4 oz)	White Wine, dry
50g (1 3/4 oz)	Onion, chopped finely
2 cloves	Garlic, whole
30-45g (1 - 1.5 oz)	Marrow (raw or prepared - see video)
60g (2 oz)	Parmesan Cheese, grated
22g (3/4 oz)	Olive Oil, extra virgin Italian
30g (1 oz)	Butter, cut in small cubes and frozen
1/4 t (0.12 g)	Saffron

PROCEDURE

1. Roast the marrow (unless you are going to use it raw).

2. Cut up and freeze the butter in small cubes.

3. Prepare the chicken stock, straining it and adding the liquid from the marrow bone to it.

4. Put the olive oil and onion into a cold pan on a MEDIUM heat. Sweat the onion for about 3 minutes.

5. Add the whole garlic cloves and the rice to the pan and cook for approximately 3 minutes, still on a medium heat.

6. When there is a nutty aroma, add the marrow and cook for another 2-3 minutes.

7. Add the white wine and continue cooking until it is nearly dry again.

8. Begin counting the critical 17 minute time as you add the first ladle of stock to the rice. Stir frequently.

9. After 4 minutes increase the heat to MEDIUM-HIGH. Continue adding stock a ladle or two at a time and stirring. Watch out there is no burning at the bottom.

10. In a separate bowl with 1-2 ladles of stock, add the saffron so that it can bloom for a few minutes.

11. Between 14 and 15 minutes after you first added stock to the rice, fish out the garlic and add the saffron-stock mixture. Continue stirring.

12. When 16 minutes have elapsed, reduce the heat back to MEDIUM and add the parmesan cheese. Stir to melt it in. If thick, add more stock.

13. On the 17 minute mark, add the frozen butter. Beat it in vigorously to emulsify. This should take roughly 45 seconds.

14. Remove the pan from the heat and cover it. Let stand covered for 5 minutes before plating.

ITALIAN MEATBALLS

This recipe was created on two continents over a period of decades from both Italian home and restaurant cooking. There is more of an art in making this than meets the eye.

INGREDIENTS

680g (24 oz)	Beef - see video for details
90g (3 oz)	Onion
90g (3 oz)	Bread Crumbs
60ml (2 oz)	Milk (or light cream)
30ml (1 oz)	Red Wine, dry
1 1/2 t	Black Peppercorns
1 1/2 t	Salt
1 t	Crushed Red Pepper Flakes (Pepperoncini)
1 t	Mustard Seeds
1 t	Marjoram
1 t	MSG (optional)
1/2 t	Fennel Seeds
5-6	Basil Leaves, fresh
400ml (14 oz)	Beef Stock (or water)
400g (14 oz)	Tomatoes, whole canned San Marzano
500g (17.5 oz)	Tomatoes, puréed (pasata)
1	Egg Yolk
1 T	Red Wine Vinegar
Garlic and Parmigiano-Reggiano	

ADDITIONAL TIPS

Deep browning of the meat is a key in maximizing flavor. Lackluster browning means lackluster flavor. The amount of time that the meatballs simmer in the sauce is also important. The best results are obtained with a low temperature for a long time. The video shows an acceptable compromise between convenience and flavor. To improve it still further, use an intense wine such as an Amarone and add some to the sauce, too.

HISTORY

This recipe is the fusion of two different styles of Italian cooking and my own experience. My first exposure to authentic Italian home cooking was back when I was in high school and my best friend was an Italian foreign exchange student. His mother and grandmother would spend all day making dinner. I also gained experience from a family member with a successful restaurant in Venice. However, local Italian critics often ridiculed that establishment as being a place for tourists rather than for carefully observing traditions. There must have been a *lot* of tourists, because every time I went there, the place was packed to capacity. Such criticism seems to run in the blood of Italian foodies.

PROCEDURE

See video, *ITALIAN MEATBALLS - Polpette in salsa di pomodoro.*

MEATLOAF OF THE GODS

Just about every culture in the world has some version of meatloaf, but this one is in the category of "none of the above", because it is a fusion of flavors and techniques from many countries and both ancient and modern times.

INGREDIENTS

450g (1 lb)	Beef, ground (see notes below)
90g (3 oz)	Onion
15g (1/2 oz)	Butter
15ml (1/2 oz)	Olive Oil
120g (4 oz)	Tomato Purée (pasata)
1 t	Paprika
3/4 t	Mustard, dry
1/2 t	Cinnamon, ground
1/4 t	Turmeric
1/2 t	Marjoram
1 t	Brown Sugar, ideally Cassonade
3/4 t	Lemon Zest
1 1/4 t	Salt
3/4 t	MSG (Accent flavor enhancer)
1/2 t	Black Pepper, ground
2 t (10 ml)	Worcestershire Sauce
1	Egg Yolk
60g (2 oz)	Breadcrumbs
45g (1.5 oz)	Cream
2 T	Parsley, freshly minced

ADDITIONAL TIPS

Grind your own beef for optimum results. If you want a more intense flavor, then reduce the amount of beef to 400 grams. This is the way that I enjoy it personally, but many find it too concentrated that way. For those who prefer a milder taste (notably French and Russians) you can increase the amount of meat to as much as 600 grams and still have good flavor. Use the sauce sparingly, or you will overpower the flavor of the meat.

<u>FOR THE CREAMY GARLIC SAUCE</u>

90g (3 oz)	Mayonnaise
60g (2 oz)	Kefir or Buttermilk
4 cloves	Garlic
15ml (1/2 oz)	Lemon Juice
1 1/2 t	Sugar
1/4 t	White Pepper
1/2 t	Salt

HISTORY

This recipe evolved slowly as the combination of several separate meatloaf and meatball recipes that I developed over the years. The unique flavor comes primarily from the seemingly unnatural combination of cinnamon and Worcestershire. This combination has its origins in ancient Rome, where garum and cinnamon were both highly regarded seasonings, and the origin of Worcestershire sauce is Roman garum, by the way.

PROCEDURE

See video, *"MEATLOAF OF THE GODS"*.

GARLIC ROASTED CHICKEN WINGS

Aside from being easy and inexpensive to prepare in large quantities, these wings are a crowd pleaser because they are crispy but not greasy, and have a great sauce-friendly flavor.

	SEASONING MIX
2 t	Garlic Powder
1 t	Onion Powder
1 t	4-Mix Peppercorns (black, white, green, pink)
1 t	Thyme
1 t	Marjoram
1/2 t	Celery, dried
1/2 t	Turmeric
1/4 t	Cumin, ground
1/4 t	Cayenne
1 1/2 t	Salt
1 t	Sugar
1	Chicken Stock cube, preferably Knorr
2 t	Flour

ADDITIONAL TIPS

You will get better results using an outdoor wood-burning grill to finish the last stage of cooking, so if you are going camping, take a box of these along with you. If you want to make a much spicier version of this same recipe, add a teaspoon or two of cayenne pepper, or much better, 2 tablespoons of Kasmiri chili powder (available in Indian spice stores). You can also use a spicy sauce, if you like. This cooking method that produces tender, moist and non-greasy wings will work with many permutations. Finally, you can also separate the wings from the drumettes after roasting, but before broiling, if desired. Keeping them together as complete wings during the roasting process will keep them moister.

HISTORY

Every nightclub in Russia has a section of the menu devoted to "beer

---

FOR THE CREAMY GARLIC SAUCE

90g (3 oz)	Mayonnaise
60g (2 oz)	Kefir or Buttermilk
4 cloves	Garlic
15ml (1/2 oz)	Lemon Juice
1 1/2 t	Sugar
1/4 t	White Pepper
1/2 t	Salt

---

snacks", which are large servings designed to by shared among several people at one table in the same way that nachos are served in Mexican restaurants. These were an instant hit!

One footnote: Dried celery doesn't exist as a seasoning in Russia, so celery leaves were dried overnight in a slow oven the same way that I describe drying chilies. Not long ago, celery stalks were not considered edible in Russia. Only the leaves were used (mostly in soups). The stalks were never sold in stores, and discarded by those who grew the plant!

PROCEDURE

See video, *Roasted Garlic Chicken Wings.*

HUNGARIAN GOULASH

First I'll say that there is no such thing as one "authentic" recipe for Hungarian anything, but I'd bet money that this is the best Goulash you'll ever taste.

GOULASH INGREDIENTS

600g (1.3 lbs)	Beef, not fatty
2 T	Hot Paprika (this is NOT Cayenne)
1 T	Sweet Paprika, best quality
1 L (1 qt)	Beef Stock, or Knorr gel (see video)
1	Yellow Bell Pepper
2	Tomatoes (150g/5 oz after peeling)
* 90ml (3 oz)	Red Wine, dry (optional)
2-3 t	Caraway Seeds
2 t	Fresh Herbs (e.g. parsley, dill, thyme)
Onions, Celery, Carrot, Garlic (see video)	
Sour Cream (for serving)	
Coarse Salt, Black Pepper	

PAPRIKA AND GOULASH HISTORY

Goulash is a very, very old dish. It was originally made with only onion and black pepper. Columbus brought paprika from the New World in the 15th century and the Turks brought it to Hungary in the 16th century. Paprika didn't become a popular ingredient in Hungary until the early 1800's, when there was a cholera epidemic and it was believed that paprika was a remedy. Then they started making everything from liquors to desserts with paprika, but after the cholera was gone, the paprika fields remained and the people had developed a taste for it. The paprika that grows in Hungary is generally regarded as the sweetest and best, due to climate and their centuries of expertise in cultivation.

CRITICISM OF THIS RECIPE

There have been several complaints that this dish is not authentic, which is also a very common complaint I hear from Italians regarding virtually every recipe posted by anyone on YouTube that claims to be Italian. Aside from regional variations, which are quite extreme in the case of both Italy and Hungary, there are major differences between homestyle and restaurant cookery, as I explained earlier in this book. Almost every recipe that I put up on YouTube is a restaurant recipe. These are almost always more complex than home recipes, include more ingredients and deliver more intense and richer flavors. The reason is because paying customers expect a better result than they obtain at home, yet when they see the recipe, the are prone to complaining that it isn't the same as a home style recipe. Quite right. It is better.

FOR CSIPETKE	
100g (3.5 oz)	Flour
1	Egg, whole
1/2 t	Salt

An exception to that rule is the Csipetke that I showed here. This is a simple, amateurish dumpling with rustic charm that is consistent with Hungarian home cooking. This is intentional as evidence to diners that this is homemade, and not something from a factory.

PROCEDURE

See video, *Best Hungarian Goulash.*

PORK BIRIYANI

Most so-called Pork Biriyani recipes are actually Chicken Biriyani recipes that have had the meat swapped. This recipe has a seasoning mixture that is optimized for the pork.

	SPICE BLEND
1 1/2 t	Coriander Seeds
1 t	Caraway Seeds
4cm (1.5 inch)	Cinnamon Stick
5	Green Cardamom pods
1	Brown Cardamom pod
2	Red Chilies, dried
3/4 t	Cloves, whole (the spice - not garlic)
1/2 t	Black Peppercorns
1/2 t	Nutmeg, ground
1/2 t	Anise Seeds
1 1/2 t	Salt
1 t	Dark Muscovado Sugar
1 t	Amchur (dried mango powder)

ADDITIONAL TIPS

Although I state that it is optional in the recipe online, for best results do not leave out the fried onions. The cashew nuts and rose water are much more a matter of personal preference. If you can get them, organic rose petals that were grown for culinary use, make an outstanding garnish in lieu of the rose water. The flashes of bright pink makes this a colorful and memorable dish, but don't use roses that were for floral bouquets because they contain pesticides. When it comes to garnishing food with fresh flowers, ideally grow them in your own garden without chemicals.

OTHER INGREDIENTS

340g (12 oz)	Pork Shoulder or neck
1 1/2 T	Ginger, grated
6 cloves	Garlic, minced
60g (2 oz)	Yogurt, whole
2-3	Green Serrano Chilies (see video)
310g (11 oz)	Basmati Rice
1/4 t	Saffron
60ml	Milk
6-8	Cherry Tomatoes, halved
2	Bay Leaves
30g (1 oz)	Ghee or clarified butter
1/2 cup	Cilantro, freshly minced
1/4 cup	Mint leaves, freshly minced
1/2	Lime (for juice)
90g (3oz)	Onions, thinly sliced and browned in oil
* 15-30g (1/2-1oz)	Cashew Nuts, fried in oil (optional)
* 1 t	Rose Water (optional)

HISTORY

Some people are surprised to see caraway seeds in an Indian recipe. These are called shah jeera in Hindi, or sometimes "white cumin", and they are a traditional ingredient, though not as common as cumin. Also, technically speaking they are not the seeds, but actually the dried fruits of the caraway plant. In Latin the words for *caraway* and *cumin* are the same, as in Russia. This is a frequent problem when attempting to purchase cumin or caraway, since the packages have identical labels and are often sealed so you can't see inside until you pay for it and open it up.

PROCEDURE

See video, *PORK BIRIYANI made in a Pressure Cooker.*

MAKHANA METHI PRAWNS

As in many of my recipes, I have tried to take the best of two related dishes and combine them into one. In this case, the fusion of a classic dish from India and a relatively recent popular street food in Malaysia. If I had to choose a single dish from this book to encourage people to try, this would be it!

INGREDIENTS

12	Prawns, very large
30g (1 oz)	Yogurt, whole
1 T	Ghee (or vegetable oil)
1 T	Lime Juice, fresh
1 1/2 T	Fenugreek Leaves, dried (methi)
1 1/2 T	Garlic, crushed
1 T	Ginger, grated
1 T	Onion, grated
1 T	Muscovado Sugar, or Coconut Sugar
1 T	Kashmiri Chili Powder (see opposing page)
3/4 t	Salt
1/2 t	White Pepper, ground
1/4 t	Turmeric
*1/2 t	MSG (Accent flavor enhancer; optional)
*few drops	Red Food Coloring (optional)
Butter, freshly chopped Cilantro and Lemon	

ADDITIONAL TIPS

Use the marinade within 30 minutes of making it. The flavor changes rapidly. Serve this with a wedge of lemon—not lime. The lime juice is for cooking, but the lemon flavor works best for the balance at the end. Be generous with the cilantro at the end. Do not substitute or leave out the fenugreek leaves (methi), as they are the basis of this recipe.

CAYENNE vs. KASHMIRI CHILI POWDER

In India, the term "chili powder" means cayenne, and it is not the same thing as Kashmiri chili powder. Unfortunately there is a lot of confusion because "chili powder" means something else in many other countries, especially the United States. Undoubtedly this is because of the popular old Western dish of simmered beans and meat with the same name. In the United States, "chili powder" means a mixture of dried chiles with other spices and herbs such as cumin and oregano, intended for making Chilli Con Carne. It is not nearly as hot as cayenne and the flavor is completely different.

Many people do not realize that cayenne is actually made from several different types of hot chili peppers that are dried, ground and then blended to produce a consistent level of heat. There is not very much flavor in cayenne—almost only heat. Conversely, Indian Kashmiri chili powder is rich in flavor, but mild in heat, although not as mild as paprika. Because genuine authentic Kashmiri chili powder can be difficult to find outside of India, a substitution is often made of half cayenne and half paprika. You can do that here if you need to.

PROCEDURE

See video, *Makhana Methi Prawns.*

CHICKEN CURRY

The varies some from the typical traditional Indian method, but this will save you some time and the result tastes absolutely authentic and delicious.

INGREDIENTS

450g (1 lb)	Chicken legs and thighs, boneless/skinless
1 t	Cumin seeds
3/4 t	Coriander, whole
1/2 t	Mace (or substitute nutmeg)
1/2 t	Mustard, dried (or seeds)
1/2 t	Turmeric
8	Allspice, whole
6	Cloves, whole (the spice - not garlic)
3 pods	Cardamom, green
2.5cm (1") piece	Cinnamon (or cassia)
1/2 (or more)	Red Chili Peppers, dried (see note below)
2 t	Sugar, preferably demerara
1 1/2 t	Salt
100g (3.5 oz)	Onions, cut in thin rings
15g (1/2 oz)	Garlic, minced
15g (1/2 oz)	Ginger, grated
200g (7 oz)	Tomatoes, Italian canned; cubed
2 t	Fenugreek Leaves, dried (methi)
100g (3.5 oz)	Coconut Cream - or Yogurt (whole)

Ghee (or vegetable oil), Cilantro, Lemon juice, Chili Oil

ADDITIONAL INFORMATION

If you want it very hot, then add more chili peppers. Use red serrano peppers that you have dried yourself for maximum flavor. Because the spices are cooked on the outside of the chicken where they are protected from burning by the moisture of the meat, there is no need to toast them separately or to marinate the chicken, which saves time. This is well suited to storing and reheating by microwave later. Remember that it will be less spicy the next day. For less calories and still an authentic taste, use yogurt in place of the coconut cream. Do not use lowfat yogurt, though.

PROCEDURE

1. In a spice grinder, combine the cumin, allspice, cloves, cardamom, cinnamon, dried chili, coriander, mace, dried mustard, turmeric, sugar and salt. Take out 2 teaspoons of the resulting powder and set it aside for use later. Pour the rest of the spice mix over the chicken thighs and coat well.

2. In a large skillet, gently fry the whole chicken pieces (don't cut them up) in a mixture of half butter and oil on a MEDIUM heat. Cook until just barely done. Set chicken aside in a bowl to collect the juices that run off.

3. In the same pan gently fry the onions, stirring frequently until they are almost golden. Add a little more oil if you have to.

4. Add the garlic and ginger. After a minute, add the 2 teaspoons of reserved spices along with the juices that ran off the chicken. Cook for 3 minutes, being careful not to burn the spices at all.

5. Now add the canned tomatoes and the dried fenugreek leaves. Increase heat to MEDIUM HIGH for 6 minutes. Reduce heat back to MEDIUM for another 6 minutes until you have a dense fragrant masala.

6. Scrape the masala into a blender along with the yogurt and a cup of water to thin it out. Blend, then pour it into a sauce pan. Cut the chicken into pieces and add them the sauce along with 3 T minced fresh cilantro. Simmer covered on a VERY LOW heat for 30 minutes. Remove lid and increase heat to MEDIUM. Stir and cook for 10-15 minutes until thick.

7. When serving, add more fresh cilantro and a squeeze of lemon juice. Also add **HOT CHILI OIL**. This is an integral part of the flavor! The recipe for it is on the next page.

HOT CHILI OIL

Just as in the case of dried chilies, most low-end restaurants buy a commercial chili oil to use. Far better results are obtained by making your own. Suddenly your Indian dish will go from being merely authentic tasting to being something fit for a Maharaja.

INGREDIENTS

50g (1.75 oz)	Red Chili Peppers (see notes below)
35g (1.25 oz)	Shallot
150g (5 oz)	Vegetable Oil
1 1/2 t	Cumin Seeds, whole
1/2 t	Paprika
1 T	Malt Vinegar, or Sherry Vinegar
1 t	Salt

ADDITIONAL TIPS

The type of chili you use is important for both the amount of heat and the flavor. Avoid jalapeño and habanero chilies because they have a distinctive flavor that is not authentic to Indian cuisine. Serrano chilies are what I use. If you want it hotter then use small Thai chilies. If you want it insanely hot, then use bhut jolokia, also known as ghost chili peppers.

STORAGE

This will keep forever without spoiling, but the amount of heat will gradually fade. You can slow this process down by storing it in the refrigerator, but even then you will find that after months it is much weaker than when it was fresh.

BHUT JOLOKIA (aka GHOST CHILIES, RED NAGA CHILIES)

While the habanero, or Scotch bonnet chili, generally is still thought of as the world's hottest chili, with a Scoville rating of 100,000 to 300,000. Officially it lost that title many years ago when laboratory testing showed that bhut jolokia could reach over 1,000,000 Scoville units. To put this in perspective, the heat of a Serrano chili is 10,000 to 25,000 on the Scoville scale. Also commonly known as ghost chilies, bhut jolokia are native to Assam, India, where they are used in making blindingly hot curries and chutneys. However, in very small amounts one can experience the novel flavor while avoiding an emergency trip to the burn ward for your tongue. Of course I'm not being serious there, because there is no actual heat. A chemical called capsaicin overloads your taste buds with a kind of physiological high voltage signal that can leave you with a diminished ability to taste anything for a short period of time. Contrary to popular belief, hot chili peppers do not kill taste buds, though. There is no permanent damage. So if the ghost chili still doesn't scare you, then try a Carolina Reaper, which is currently the hottest known chili pepper in the world. In 2014, one of these peppers was scientifically measured to have a Scoville rating of more than 2,000,000. Unless you are really into seriously hot food, stick to Serrano chilies. The flavor is a good match for most Indian dishes, and you can control the amount of heat easier. When you have a chili oil with the strength of nitroglycerine, a couple of extra drops takes it from being merely painful to being completely inedible.

PROCEDURE

See video, *HOT CHILI OIL for PROFESSIONAL INDIAN Curry.*

BAINGAN BHARTA (EGGPLANT CURRY)

Authentic recipes for this wonderful vegetarian Punjabi dish are seldom seen. I created this one from combined experience.

INGREDIENTS

700g (1.5 lbs)	Eggplant (2 medium sized)
200g (7 oz)	Tomato Purée (pasata)
180g (6.3 oz)	Coconut Milk (canned is okay)
120g (4.2 oz)	Onion, sliced in thin rings
45g (1.5 oz)	Ghee or clarified butter
1-2	Green Serrano Chilies. diced
2 T	Ginger, freshly grated
6 cloves	Garlic, chopped
1-2 T	Brown Sugar, ideally Cassonade (to taste)
1 pod	Brown Cardamom
2 t	Coriander Seeds
1 1/2 t	Mustard Seeds
1/2 t	Cloves (the spice)
2.5cm (1") piece	Cinnamon stick
1/2 t	Black Peppercorns
1/2 - 3/4 t	Garam Masala (see index)

Cilantro, Cream (or yogurt), Lemon wedges

ADDITIONAL INFORMATION

The process of salting eggplant was originally to draw out the bitterness, but modern eggplants have been selectively bred so that they aren't bitter. When you salt them like this, the purpose is to increase the texture so that pieces don't turn to gelatinous mush. Ideally you want to roast the eggplant in a wood burning oven. Fresh coconut milk makes this dish even better, but in restaurants we usually rely on the canned product.

PROCEDURE

1. Peel the eggplants and cut them into 2.5cm (1") thick slices. Salt them on both sides and place the pieces between sheets of paper towel. Change the paper after 15 minutes. Preheat oven to 210°C (410°F).

2. After another 15-20 minutes, wipe the excess salt from each slice of eggplant and coat it with vegetable oil. Line up the slices on a baking sheet. Roast for 25 minutes, then turn pieces over and roast another 10-15 minutes. Remove from the oven and leave to cool down for 2-3 hours.

3. In a hot pan, lightly toast the brown cardamom, coriander seeds, cloves, mustard seeds and cinnamon stick until the mustard seeds start to pop. Combine in a spice grinder along with the black peppercorns. Pass the resulting powder through a fine mesh sieve to remove any large bits.

4. Gently fry the onion in the ghee (or clarified butter) on MEDIUM (#5 out of 10) until turning golden (12-15 minutes), stirring frequently.

5. Add the garlic, ginger and green chilies. Cook for 3 minutes on the same heat setting. Now add the spice mixture and stir. Cook for 1 minute, then add the tomato purée and the sugar. About 5 minutes later, add 3 T of cilantro stems (washed and chopped). Continue cooking with frequent stirring until you have a very thick masala. Reduce heat slightly as it thickens. Don't rush it! When it is nearly done, add the Garam Masala.

6. Add the coconut milk and 90ml (3 oz) of water. Stir to combine. At this point you can purée the mixture in a blender for a smoother result, or leave it with more texture. The choice is yours, but I suggest blending it.

7. If you did blend it, now return the curry to the pan. Cut each slice of eggplant into large pieces and add them to the pan. Stir and simmer covered on a LOW heat (#3) for 10-15 minutes. Remove the lid and add cream (or yogurt) to taste. Also add more salt, if needed. Serve with more fresh cilantro, paper thin slices of onion and lemon wedges on the side.

105

SWEET & SMOKY CHICKEN WINGS

This recipe has stood the test of time—and of geography, being extremely popular everywhere in the world that I have put it on the menu now for years. This is the first time that I have shared the recipe publicly.

INGREDIENTS FOR GLAZE

600ml (21 oz)	Pineapple Juice, ideally Dole
75g (2.5 oz)	Onion, chopped medium
30ml (1 oz)	Vegetable Oil
250g (9 oz)	Tomato Purée (pasata)
15g (1/2 oz)	Garlic, chopped
150g (5.3 oz)	Sugar
110ml (3.9 oz)	Apple Cider Vinegar
1 1/2 t	Salt
30g (1 oz)	Ketchup
1 t	Cayenne
15-20ml (3-4 t)	Liquid Smoke

ADDITIONAL TIPS

The reduction requires careful monitoring near the end. It will go from being too thin to burnt in a surprisingly short period of time. Lower the heat as it gets close to being finished. In restaurants, we lose many batches from careless cooks who thought they could step away.

What is convenient about this recipe is that you can make up the glaze up to a week ahead of time. Then you deep fry the chicken and toss the cooked pieces in a bowl with the glaze straight out of the refrigerator. The heat from the fried chicken will melt the glaze, producing glossy and deeply flavored wings anytime you want them.

106

PROCEDURE FOR THE GLAZE

1. Heat a large sauce pan or a stock pot. Add the vegetable oil and cook the onion on a MEDIUM heat until it just starts to turn golden.

2. Add the tomato purée and the garlic. Cook for about 5 minutes until thick.

3. Add the pineapple juice, sugar, apple cider vinegar and salt. Bring up to a strong simmer (80-90°C, or about 185°F), stirring occasionally. Continue reducing until the sauce starts to get thick and darkens. Watch carefully for this stage so that you don't burn it. This will take careful attention, judgement and some experience to get perfect.

4. Add the ketchup and the cayenne. Cook another few minutes until thicker. Remove from the heat and add the liquid smoke. Refrigerate.

PROCEDURE FOR THE CHICKEN WINGS

1. Divide the chicken wings into wingettes and drummetes. Dust with a little thyme, white pepper and flour. Only use a little flour, as you do not want them gummy.

2. Deep fry at 160°C (320°F) for about 7 minutes, or until golden and cooked through.

3. Drain the pieces and put them in a bowl containing some of the glaze. Toss to coat.

4. Serve with DIPPING SAUCE, made by whisking together...

FOR DIPPING SAUCE

170g (6 oz)	Mayonnaise
100g (3.5 oz)	Kefir, or Buttermilk
50ml (1.75 oz)	Lemon Juice
1 T	Sugar

CHIMICHANGAS

I turned this Arizona Tex-Mex classic into a Russian bar snack with great success. These are incredibly addictive, and my innovation here of using lavash for the wrapper that creates a light and flaky pastry takes them to a whole new level.

INGREDIENTS

340g (12 oz)	Ground Pork
240g (8.5 oz)	White Beans, canned (rinsed)
30g (1 oz)	Garlic, chopped
2	Jalapeño Chili Peppers
90g (3.2 oz)	Onion, diced
1 T	Cumin, ground
30g (1 oz)	Ketchup
2 t	Salt
1 t	Black Pepper
1 t	MSG
3 T	Cilantro, minced

Lavash (see notes below), Egg

ADDITIONAL NOTES

Because there are no real tortillas available in Russia, or even masa in which to make your own tortillas, I tried using lavash. This is a thin flatbread from Armenia that is popular in Turkey and the Middle East— and happens to be readily available in Russia. To my surprise, this actually works better than tortillas. The light, crisp and flaky texture that results from deep frying these is perfect. Select a brand of lavash that is very thin.

PROCEDURE FOR THE FILLING

1. Fry the ground pork in a small stock pot on a HIGH heat (#8 out of 10), along with the cumin and salt until no longer pink.

2. Add the onion, garlic, green chili and black pepper. Reduce heat to MEDIUM (#5 out of 10). Cook for 10 minutes, stirring occasionally.

3. Add the drained white beans, ketchup and MSG. Cook 5 more minutes.

4. Add the cilantro, then transfer to a food processor. Pulse a few times to an even consistency, but do not turn it into a purée. You want pieces.

FIRE AND ICE DIPPING SAUCE

45ml (1,5 oz)	Vegetable Oil
140g (10.5 oz)	Tomato Purée (pasata)
60g (3 oz)	Onion
2	Red Serrano Chilies
15g (1/2 oz)	Garlic
2 t	Paprika
90ml (3 oz)	Apple Cider Vinegar
1 t	Cumin, ground
1 t	Salt
Smetana (or Sour Cream)	

PROCEDURE FOR THE SAUCE

1. Heat a sauce pan on a VERY HIGH heat (#9 out of 10). Add the tomato purée all at once. Do not stir, and watch out for splattering! Sprinkle the paprika and salt to the bubbling tomato sauce.

2. When the steam subsides and the mixture starts to thicken, add the onion, garlic, red chilies and cumin. Reduce heat to MEDIUM and stir.

3. When very thick add the vinegar. Allow it to stand until it cools to room temperature, stirring occasionally. Blend to a purée.

ASSEMBLY

Wrap the filling in squares of lavash, sealing with beaten egg. Deep fry at 180°C (350°F) until golden brown. Serve with sauce and sour cream.

RIBEYE STEAK SCHI

Traditional Schi is one of the staples of most Russian households. It is a cabbage soup that includes potatoes, mushrooms and sometimes a little meat. My version was created for a Russian restaurant with a western theme, but it was important for them to have dishes on the menu that Russian customers could relate to. This became a very popular item, especially in the cold winter months.

INGREDIENTS

300g (10.6 oz)	Ribeye Steak
750ml (26.5 oz)	Beef Stock
100g (3.5 oz)	Red Onion, diced medium
70g (2.5 oz)	Carrot, grated
125g (4.4 oz)	Potato, diced
125g (4.4 oz)	Brussels Sprouts, sliced
100g (3.5 oz)	Mushrooms, preferably wild
1 t	Cumin seeds, whole
1 whole	Bay Leaf
30g (1 oz)	Ketchup
1 t	Sharena Sol (see index)

Butter, Olive Oil, and Sour Cream for serving

ADDITIONAL TIPS

The beef stock you use for this does not require an especially refined product. Brown some beef bones and scraps, then simmer with water, carrot, onion and celery for several hours. Remove the solids and pass the broth through a sieve. A simple stock like this really only takes a few minutes of actual cooking time. Start this sort of thing early in the morning and leave it to simmer on a back burner until you use it later that day.

PROCEDURE

1. Season steak well on both sides with coarse salt and freshly ground black pepper. Coat with olive oil and grill (or fry) to develop a good brown crust, taking care not to actually burn the meat.

2. Set meat aside for now. In the same hot pan, add the onions. Stir for a couple of minutes until the onion softens, then add the cumin seeds and toast them for about a minute.

3. Add the beef stock. Then add the steak (whole) with the carrot, the bay leaf and 1/2 teaspoon of ground black pepper. Partially cover and bring to a slow simmer and cook for 2 hours, stirring occasionally.

4. Remove the meat and the bay leaf. Discard the bay and let the meat cool on a plate. Now add the potato and simmer for 10 more minutes.

5. During this time, fry the mushrooms in a little butter. Drain off the butter and add the mushrooms to the soup.

6. Cut the steak up into pieces, taking care to discard any large pieces of fat or gristle, then add that to the soup along with the Brussels sprouts, ketchup and Sharena Sol. Simmer about 20 minutes longer. To serve, add a small dollop of sour cream topped with a sprig of dill.

EMIRATI ROAST CAMEL

If you can't get camel meat, don't worry because this works great with beef, too. This is regarded as a dish for holidays, weddings and special occasions in the Middle East. I implore you to try this. The flavor is unique and delicious!

INGREDIENTS

700g (1.5 lbs)	Camel (or beef), cut in large cubes
70g (2.5 oz)	Red Onion, chopped (do not substitute)
1 T	Flour
2 whole	Dried Sweet Red Chilies (remove stems)
1/2	Dried Red Serrano Chili
3/4 t	Fenugreek
3/4 t	Cumin Seeds
1/2 t	Black Peppercorns, whole
2 pods	Green Cardamom, whole
2 t	Salt
90g (3.2 oz)	Tomatoes, puréed (pasata)
6 cloves	Garlic, chopped
1/2 t	Sugar
1 t	Orange Peel, dried
1/2 t	Turmeric
2 T	Yogurt, whole
250g (8.8 oz)	Basmati Rice
45g (1.5 oz)	Raisins, golden

ADDITIONAL TIPS

Camel tastes like a cross between beef and lamb, but lamb doesn't work as well here. Camel meat is available online in the USA, and at some butcher shops in Australia and Britain. Look for evenly striated muscle and remove any tough ligaments and connective tissue that won't break down. Refer to my notes earlier in this book on the dried chili peppers (see index).

PROCEDURE

1. Crush the green cardamom pods with the side of a knife and remove the small round seeds. Discard the husks. In a spice grinder, combine the seeds with the dried chilies, the fenugreek, cumin seeds, and black peppercorns. Mix this with the flour and salt in a bowl. Put the cubed meat in the bowl and massage the mixture into it, coating evenly.

2. Heat 2 T olive oil in a large heavy skillet and brown the meat in two batches. Brown very well on all sides using a HIGH heat (#8 out of 10 on the stove burner setting). Very good browning is essential to the flavor.

3. Remove the meat to a covered braising vessel as you brown it off. Lower the heat to MEDIUM (#5 out of 10). Add the onions to the hot pan that the meat was browned in and fry for about 3 minutes.

4. Add the tomato purée and cook another 3 minutes until thick. Add the garlic, sugar, dried orange peel and turmeric. Cook for 2 minutes, then add the yogurt and 150ml (5.3 oz) water. Increase heat and bring to a simmer for 4-5 minutes to thicken a bit.

5. Pour the liquid into the braising dish over the meat, distributing as evenly as possible. Cover and braise at 140°C (285°F) for 3 1/2 hours.

6. Remove from the oven and allow to cool for 30 minutes before removing the cubes of meat. If desired, strain off some of the oil from the liquid left behind before proceeding (normally the fat is all included). Add enough water to bring the total weight to 550 grams (19.4 oz). Put into a sauce pan and add the basmati rice and raisins. Bring to a simmer and cover. Reduce heat cook 15-20 minutes until done. Serve the meat on top of the rice along with thin slices of raw red onion. You may also garnish with fresh mint, cilantro and lemon wedges, if desired.

BAVARIAN PIZZA

I created this specifically for a restaurant in Berlin, Germany. This is quite different from any pizza you have ever tried, but the sales figures speak for themselves as to how delicious it is. Even though it was rather outrageously priced at around €15 (US $20) for a small 23cm (9 inch) pizza, it remains one of the most popular items on the menu.

<u>CRUST</u>

30g (1 oz)	Yeast, fresh (see notes below)
350ml (12.3 oz)	Water, luke warm
250g (8.8 oz)	Rye Flour
300g (10.6 oz)	Flour (regular All Purpose)
1 t	Salt

THE CRUST

This is about the most unorthodox pizza crust ever. The fact that I am still calling it "pizza" is sure to offend almost every Italian, so don't think of it as pizza, if that bothers you.

As for any other pizza dough, begin by dissolving the yeast in the warm water. If you can't get fresh yeast, then proof a packet of instant yeast with a little sugar in the water. Now add all of the rye flour, half of the white flour and the salt. Use the dough hook on a stand mixer to knead for 10 minutes. Add another 100g (3.5 oz) of white flour and the dough should come together over the next few minutes of kneading. Turn off the mixer and add the last of the flour to the bowl, kneading by hand. Cover with a damp towel and allow to stand at room temperature for 2 hours. Now refrigerate in a container with a tiny vent for 2 days or more. Roll out pieces very thin (use more flour) and cut them into circles using a pan lid as a template. Carefully scrape the dough off the counter using the edge of a knife. This will take practice to do cleanly. Heat 2cm (3/4 inch) oil in a frying pan to 200°C (390°F) and fry crusts until golden and crisp, turning every 30 seconds (about 2 minutes total cooking time each)..

TOPPING BASE

300g (10.6 oz)	Cabbage
200g (7 oz)	Onion
500ml (17.6 oz)	Märzen Beer (ideally Ayinger or Distelhäuser)
2 T	Dill, freshly minced (or 1 t dried)
1 T	Garlic, crushed
1 1/2 t	Black Pepper, ground
1 3/4 t	Salt

THE TOPPING

Heat 2 tablespoons of oil in a stock pot. Add the onion to it and sauté until it softens on MEDIUM-HIGH (#6 of 10). Add the cabbage, all of the salt and half of the black pepper, and begin cooking, stirring occasionally. After the cabbage is soft (10 minutes), add half the beer. Cook to evaporate it to nearly dry (20 minutes) before adding the rest of the beer, the garlic, the dill and the rest of the black pepper. Cook 15-20 minutes more until very thick. Refrigerate before use.

THE PIZZA

Smear some topping onto a previously fried crust. Add a little grated Kostromskoy cheese (or Monterey Jack), fresh mozzarella, smoked bratwurst or kielbasa slices and a lot of freshly grated Parmegiano-Regianno. Either bake in a 210°C (410°F) oven for 6-7 minutes, or (better) cook in a Josper charcoal burning oven. Garnish with finely diced tomato.

FRENCH CHICKEN AND MUSHROOMS WITH MIDDLE EASTERN SPICES

The influx of Middle Eastern immigrants to France in recent years has generated an increased appreciation for exotic spices that were previously scarce in French cuisine. Conversely, mushrooms are rarely seen in Middle Eastern cuisine.

INGREDIENTS

2	Chicken Crowns (or whole chickens)
250g (8.75 oz)	Mushrooms, champignons
45ml (1.5 oz)	Vermouth, dry
5 pods	Green Cardamom
1/2	Dried Sweet Red Chili
1/2	Dried Hot Red Chili (Serrano)
2.5cm (1")	Cinnamon stick
1 t	Cumin Seeds, whole
1 t	Ginger, dried and ground
3/4 t	Paprika
1 t	Coarse Salt
3-4 cloves	Garlic, whole
2 t	Dried Rose Buds or Petals

Carrots, Zucchini, Butter, Cilantro or Parsley

ADDITIONAL TIPS

Boneless, skin-on chicken breasts are cut from either crowns or whole chickens. Make sure they each weigh about 170 grams (6 oz). Either select large mushrooms and quarter them, or use smaller mushrooms whole. Dried rosebuds or petals are available online or in specialty Middle Eastern grocery stores. Culinary-grade roses are about 10 times stronger in flavor than bouquet roses, and they have no pesticides on them.

PROCEDURE

1. On a hot pan, toast the cardamom pods, the dried red chili and the cinnamon stick fairly aggressively. Set aside. Now toast the cumin seeds for only 15-20 seconds until they just darken, taking care not to burn them. In a spice grinder, combine these with the hot chili, cinnamon stick, cumin seeds, paprika, ginger and salt. Pass through a sieve and discard chunks.

2. Grind the sweet red chili with the rose buds or petals. Set aside.

3. Take the chicken breasts off the bone and pound to tenderize. Put one fourth of rose petal and sweet chili mixture on the inside of each breast. Add salt. Roll into cylinders with cling film and refrigerate to firm up.

4. Roast the carcass/bones in a 210°C (410°F) oven for about 30 minutes, turning occasionally. Pour off any fat, then deglaze the roasting pan with the vermouth. Set aside.

5. Coat the chicken breasts with the spice mixture. Heat 30g (1 oz) butter in a skillet on a MEDIUM-HIGH setting (#6) with the garlic cloves. Cook the mushrooms until they have absorbed most of the fat. Now add the roasting juices that were deglazed with vermouth and any extra spice mix. Add the roasted chicken bones to the pan. Cover and continue simmering for 30 minutes. Then turn off the heat, remove the lid and let them dry.

7. Gently cook slices of carrot in butter. When they are about half done, add the zucchini. Add a splash of chicken stock if you have it on hand.

8. In a 210°C (410°F) preheated oven, roast the chicken for 16 minutes, then let it cool for 10 minutes more before slicing medallions.

9. To plate, place the chicken and vegetables around, finishing with the finely diced tomato for color, if desired. Add sprigs of cilantro or parsley.

TAJIKI SHASHLIK

This is basically the same as Russian shashlik, only with the addition of spices from Tajikistan and a sauce that was developed for a popular restaurant in Russia. Don't let the simplicity of this recipe deceive you. It is a perennial favorite.

INGREDIENTS

450g (1 lbs)	Lamb meat, cubed
120g (4.25 oz)	Onion, sliced
2 T	Tajiki Spice Blend (see index)
45ml (1.5 oz)	Lemon Juice, fresh

ADDITIONAL TIPS

For the best quality, cut lamb meat from rib chops and use a Jaccard device to further tenderize it. I realize that the sauce is not even close to something authentic, as well as bordering on being downright culturally offensive, but in a restaurant we are concerned with finding the optimum balance between great taste, ease of preparation and cost effectiveness. This sauce works extremely well. Just don't tell anyone what's in it.

PROCEDURE

1. Sprinkle the spice mixture on the meat and rub it in to distribute.

2. Layer the seasoned meat in a storage container with slices of onion interspersed between it. Add the lemon juice, seal the container and shake it to distribute evenly. Refrigerate for between 2 and 24 hours.

3. Put the meat on skewers and let it stand at room temperature to warm up. This will make it more tender. The onions may be either discarded, or fried well in oil as an accompaniment, or used in making a delicious soup

with fennel and garlic that I will detail in a video in the future.

4. Rub the meat with vegetable oil and grill over charcoal. Alternatively, roast for 8-10 minutes in a 220°C (430°F) oven, depending on how big the cubes of meat are and how well done you like it. You can roast some tomatoes at the same time. Thread cherry tomatoes on the skewers between the pieces of meat.

SAUCE

60g (2 oz)	Ketchup
60g (2 oz)	Mayonnaise
30g (1 oz)	Heinz 57 sauce
2 t	Garlic, crushed
15ml (1/2 oz)	Lemon Juice, fresh
1/2 t	Tabasco sauce
1/2 t	Salt

5. Try serving it with this sauce on the side (simply mix the ingredients together), as well as sprigs of fresh herbs such as mint, cilantro, parsley, sorrel and dill.

POLLO CON SAPORE CAMPANIA

This is based on a dish from a village in Campania. I have substituted readily-available kielbasa for the obscure regional sausage, and the result is a hearty crowd pleaser. It is reminiscent of the New Orleans classic, Poulet Tchoupitoulas.

INGREDIENTS

450g (1 lb)	Chicken, boneless (see notes below)
450g (1 lb)	Potatoes, waxy whiite variety
90g (3.2 oz)	Kielbasa Sausage, lightly smoked
60g (2 oz)	Red Onion, diced
3-4 cloves	Garlic, coarsely chopped
6-8	Cherry Tomatoes, halved
3/4 t	Marjoram, dried
1/2 t	Black Peppercorns
1/2 t	Crushed Red Pepper Flakes (Pepperoncini)
1 1/4 t	Salt
1 T	Flour
45ml (1.5 oz)	Red Wine Vinegar
2 t	Rosemary, freshly minced
2 T	Olive Oil

ADDITIONAL TIPS

I suggest using boneless, skinless chicken leg and thigh meat. Leaving the skin on will produce a rather heavy and greasy dish. If you want to make this with chicken breast, then pound the breast pieces well first before sectioning to help keep them tender.

The real magic in this dish happens in the last few seconds when you add in the minced rosemary. Getting the potatoes cooked to just the right consistency is paramount, and it will take some practice.

PROCEDURE

1. Cut the chicken up into 4cm (1.5 inch) cubes. In a spice grinder, combine the marjoram, black peppercorns, red pepper flakes and salt. Mix this with the flour and then coat the chicken pieces with it evenly. Allow to stand for 10-15 minutes.

2. Peel the potatoes and cut them into 2cm (3/4 inch) dice. Boil in salted water for about 5 minutes until just starting to soften. Drain and set aside.

3. Heat the olive oil up in a large skillet. Dice the kielbasa into 1.25cm (1/2 inch) cubes. Fry in the olive oil on a HIGH heat for 2-3 minutes, then add the chicken pieces. Cook until starting turn golden on all sides.

4. Reduce the heat to MEDIUM and add the onion and cherry tomatoes. Cook until the vegetables are softened (about 4-5 minutess).

5. Add the wine vinegar and the garlic. Reduce heat to LOW. Cook until the strong vinegar aroma has faded (about 2-3 minutes), stirring occasionally.

6. Put the cooked potatoes over the top of the mixture and cover. Continue cooking with the lid on at a LOW heat (#3 out of 10) for about 15 minutes.

7. Remove the lid to stir everything around. Put the lid back on and continue cooking for another 10-15 minutes, stirring from time to time.

8. Turn the heat off. Sprinkle on the finely minced rosemary and stir. Cover the pan again and leave to infuse and cool for 5 minutes before serving. Grilled or steamed artichokes make an ideal accompaniment.

CAJUN CASSOULET

The French have Cassoulet and the Cajuns have Sausage and Red Beans. This is a fusion of the two, which is a natural since Cajuns are descendents of French immigrants. Like all good fusion dishes, it is greater than the sum of its parts.

INGREDIENTS

600g (1.3 lb)	Pork Roast, not too lean
250g (8.8 oz)	Smoked Kielbasa Sausage, sliced
1-2	Confit Duck Legs (optional)
250g (8.8 oz)	Kidney Beans, dry
130g (3.5 oz)	Green Bell Pepper, diced
80g (2.8 oz)	Celery, diced
45g (1.5 oz)	Shallot or Red Onion, diced
6 cloves	Garlic, diced
1	Green Serrano Chili, freshly diced
1 T	Bacon Grease (or substitute oil)
2	Bay Leaves
2 T	Parsley, fresh
1 full recipe	Cajun Spice Blend (see index)

ADDITIONAL TIPS

If you try using canned kidney beans, they will be a pile of mush by the end. By par-boiling dry beans, they will be just tender when the rest is done. Do not select pork that is very lean, or it will be dry and chewy in the end. I suggest not using Andouile sausage, because that takes it too far in the direction of Cajun flavors. The beauty of this is in the fusion.

PROCEDURE

1. Soak the beans overnight in plain cold water.

2. Put the kidney beans into a pot containing 1.5 liters (34 oz) of cold

water and the bay leaves, but <u>no</u> salt. Heat to a simmer, and maintain gently bubbling for 1 1/2 to 2 hours, until tender. Turn off the heat and leave the beans in the hot water while you proceed.

2. Prepare the Cajun Spice blend by grinding together all of the ingredients in an electric spice mill.

3. Cut the pork into 5cm (2") cubes. Put in a bowl and mix with entire amount of the spice blend. Rub to coat as evenly as possible. Allow to stand for 15-30 minutes.

4. Heat bacon grease or oil in a skillet and gently brown the cubes of meat on a MEDIUM (#5 out of 10) heat. Do not burn the spices. This should take about 6-7 minutes, turning the pieces as you go. Set the meat off to the side.

5. Deglaze the pan with the wine, then immediately add the green bell pepper, celery, shallot, chili pepper and garlic. Stir and cook at the same heat setting for another 6-7 minutes.

6. Drain the kidney beans, reserving 100ml (3.5 oz) of the cooking liquid. Discard the bay leaves. Add the beans into the skillet with the vegetables and mix together. Put this in the bottom of a large braising dish. Over the top of the beans, add the browned pork, sliced sausage and confit duck (if you're using it).

7. Braise at 140°C (285°F) for 2 1/2 hours.

8. Allow to cool for 30 minutes. Plate with a little freshly minced parsley. Russians eat this with bread that has been spread with mayonnaise instead of butter. Garlic aioli is also excellent. Unless you absolutely hate mayo, be sure to try this!

⟡

STUFFED BUTTERNUT SQUASH

This is a great holiday dish, and it can be prepared ahead of time and just put in the oven to finish whenever you need it.

INGREDIENTS

1	Butternut Squash, medium size
120g (4 oz)	Onion
60g (2 oz)	Bacon
60g (2 oz)	Dates, pitted
30ml (1 oz)	Mosto Cotto, or substitute Balsamic Vinegar
3/4 t	Thyme, dried
1	Egg Yolk
1-2 T	Bread Crumbs
30g (1 oz)	Walnuts
1 T	Thyme, fresh

Coarse Salt, Cracked Black Pepper

MOSTO COTTO

Mosto Cotto is the reduction of a type of grape juice that is the first step in making true Balsamic vinegar. There are different types of Mosto Cotto that range from tasting extremely sweet to being rather sour. You want one in the middle with a balance of sweet and sour tastes. My favorite for this is *Conte de Bellomonte*, from Italy. This is difficult to find, though. You can substitute commercial Balsamic vinegar and still have acceptable results.

ADDITIONAL NOTES

The quality of the butternut squash you use for this is will make all the difference, and this is something that is frequently overlooked because squash tends to look good physically until it is just about completely rancid. Try to get the best farm fresh squash that you can.

For scaling up the recipe, simply multiply all of the ingredients by the number of squash you will be preparing. You might also consider substituting cilantro for the fresh thyme that is mixed with the walnuts for the topping, but this will depend entirely on what you plan to serve it with. The same is true of the black pepper. The amount you add will have a great influence on the character of this dish, and what it compliments.

ROASTING THE SQUASH

1. Cut off the stem end of the squash, then slice it lengthwise in two. Scoop out the seeds, but don't remove any of the flesh. Rub with vegetable oil on both sides, then place cut-side down on a baking sheet sprinkled with coarse salt. Roast until tender, as explained in the video.

2. Allow it to cool completely down to room temperature. This will take several hours. You may refrigerate it after it reaches room temperature and continue the next day with perfectly good results. The cooling stage is important, not only with this dish, but with butternut squash in general. The best results are obtains by first roasting, letting it cool, then continuing on with whatever preparation you have in mind for it, even if you are only making a simple soup.

PROCEDURE FOR THE FILLING AND COOKING

See video, *Stuffed Butternut Squash*

CHICKEN SATAY

While this is usually thought of as a Thai dish, the reality is that it is that its roots are in the Middle East, Singapore and India. Each region has their own variations. I've combined the ideas that I like from several different sources to produce a recipe that has wide general appeal, which is the goal of good restaurant recipes, of course.

INGREDIENTS

350g (12.3 oz)	Chicken, boneless skinless thighs/legs
45g	Peanut Butter
1 T	Galangal, grated (or young ginger)
1 T	Garlic, crushed
1 T	Soy Sauce, dark
1 T	Coconut Milk, or Yogurt, whole
1 T	Brown Sugar, ideally Date Palm
2 t	Lemongrass, minced (see note below)
1 t	Turmeric
1/2 t	Coriander seeds, ground
1/2 t	Sesame Oil
1/2 t	Garam Masala (see notes below)
1/4 t	Liquid Smoke
1/4 t	Cayenne

VARIATIONS

Personally I prefer yogurt this, though coconut milk is more traditional. The use of Garam Masala in the marinade is not mentioned in the video, but it is something to try out if you like Satay. Be sure to use the Garam Masala that you prepare yourself (see index of this book). The liquid smoke is not necessary if grilling over wood, which is by far the best way to cook this. The oven is very much a second choice.

ADDITIONAL NOTES

Lemongrass is difficult to find sometimes, and I have made this with cilantro roots and obtained very good results. The same thing goes for substituting ginger for galangal. It isn't ideal, but the result is still

<table>
<tr><td colspan="2" align="center"><u>SAUCE</u></td></tr>
<tr><td>45g (1.5 oz)</td><td>Peanut Butter</td></tr>
<tr><td>45g (1.5 oz)</td><td>Coconut Milk, or Yogurt, whole</td></tr>
<tr><td>15ml (1/2 oz)</td><td>Lime Juice</td></tr>
<tr><td>2 t</td><td>Sugar (white)</td></tr>
<tr><td>1 t</td><td>Soy Sauce</td></tr>
<tr><td>1 t</td><td>Sesame Oil</td></tr>
<tr><td>1/2 t</td><td>Nam Pla (Thai Fish Sauce)</td></tr>
<tr><td>1/4 t</td><td>Salt</td></tr>
</table>

delicious. If you have a choice, get young ginger (visibly much smaller in size) because the taste is even closer to galangal.

PRESENTATION

To prepare the sauce, simply microwave the peanut butter to soften it, then whisk all of the ingredients together. Serve with sprigs of fresh cilantro, thin slices of red chilies, wedges of lime, and the sauce on the side.

PROCEDURE

See video, *Chicken Satay.*

ROAST DUCK

Every serious cook should know how to roast a duck perfectly. Here are clear directions, and if you use this seasoning, you are sure to get rave reviews.

INGREDIENTS

2kg (4.4 lb)	Duck, whole (frozen and defrosted is okay)
30g (1 oz)	Hofbrau Seasoning (see index)
1	Orange
about 1/2 t	Angostura bitters

PROCEDURE

1. Preheat oven to 190°C (390°F) with fan assist on. If you don't have fan assist, then preheat to 205°C (400°F), and the results won't be as good.

2. Rinse and dry the duck. Prick holes in the skin where the legs and thighs join, and around the breasts. Put about half of the Hofbrau seasoning inside the cavity. Now cut the orange into quarters and sprinkle the pieces with Angostura bitters. Stuff the orange pieces inside the cavity. Put the duck on a roasting rack and sprinkle with the rest of the seasoning on both sides as evenly as possible. Roast for 1 hour and 30 minutes (adjust time for different weight ducks, subtracting or adding 1 minute for every 25g / 1 oz. difference from the size specified here.

3. Remove from oven and tent with foil for 15 minutes. Remove foil tent and let it stand for another 15-30 minutes before removing the orange pieces from inside and cutting to serve.

4. Sprinkle a little more of the Hofbrau seasoning on as you are serving it.

GLAZED VEGETABLES

This is another technique that every serious cook should master as a nearly universal plating element, as well as a side dish. This is a skill you will have to practice some.

INGREDIENTS

Vegetables - one type per pan (see notes below)
Veal, Chicken or Duck Stock
Sugar
Butter
Sprigs of Thyme or other herb (optional)

NOTES

Vegetables cook at different rates so you generally need a separate pan for each vegetable. This method can be used for potatoes and other long-cooking vegetables, but you have to cut them into smaller pieces.

PROCEDURE

1. Cut vegetables in uniform size pieces so that they cook at the same rate. Use a pan large enough to hold all of the pieces in a single layer without very much extra space. Add the weight of the vegetables in veal or chicken stock, then enough water to just cover the vegetables. Now add a little sugar (about a teaspoon per 120g/4.2 oz of vegetables), salt, a knob of butter, and the fresh herb if you are using that.

2. Heat to a simmer. Reduce liquid until nearly dry, being careful not to scorch the vegetables. Stir occasionally with a rubber spatula. If the vegetables are still not tender, add more water and repeat the reduction.

BLUEBERRY MUFFINS

I normally leave desserts up to the pastry chef, but every serious cook needs to master at least a few baked goods. This is one that is sure to impress anyone. They taste at least as good the next day, so you can make them in advance.

INGREDIENTS

120g (4.25 oz)	Butter, cold (cut into cubes)
120g (4.25 oz)	Sugar
2 whole	Eggs
150g (5.3 oz)	Kefir, 2.5% fat (or buttermilk)
150g (5.3 oz)	Flour
1 1/2 t	Baking Powder
1/2 t	Baking Soda
1/4 t	Salt
75g (2.75 oz)	Blueberries, ideally fresh
1 T	Powdered Sugar

BAKER'S FRUIT TRICK

Although this is common knowledge among bakers, many have not heard of this. When you start making this, get a bowl and toss the blueberries with the powdered sugar. Bump them around a bit until they get bruised and a bit sticky. When it comes time to add them to the batter, add a little flour and give them a final toss. This will help to keep the berries from sinking to the bottom of the muffin during cooking. Then they will be more evenly distributed and give you a professional result. You can use frozen blueberries, but the result will not be as good.

ADDITIONAL TIPS

These are just the right sweetness for muffins, but not very sweet for a cupcake. You can frost them to turn them into a dessert.

PROCEDURE

1. Preheat oven to 180°C (355°F). Cream the butter, sugar and salt in a stand mixer with the paddle attachment.

2. Add the eggs, kefir (or buttermilk) and baking powder. Run the mixer slowly at first, then a bit faster for about a minute in all.

3. Add the flour and baking soda (premix the two) as the mixer is running, being careful not to let it fly out by adding it too quickly. Run the mixer to make it smooth, but don't over mix it.

4. Remove the bowl from the mixer and fold in the blueberries by hand with a spatula.

5. Butter six silicone muffin molds well as a precaution against sticking. You can use paper liners if you want to. Divide the mixture into the cups evenly.

6. Bake for 32-42 minutes. The exact time will vary some due to many factors including the type of kefir or buttermilk, the size eggs, how fresh the blueberries were, your altitude, how accurate your oven thermostat is, etc. Keep notes on exactly what you did and adjust the baking time for the next batch. Such is the nature of professional baking if you want perfection.

7. Cool the silicone mold on a wire rack for 30 minutes before carefully unmolding. Allow the muffins to rest on the wire rack until they reach room temperature. While they are good fresh, most people agree that they are far better the next day. Try butter or cream cheese on them with breakfast.

Spice Blends

There are two shortcuts to unique flavors in what you cook. One is the sauce and the other is the spice blend. The success of Kentucky Fried Chicken stands as proof of what the right blend of herbs and spices can accomplish. Here are five useful blends that produce unique flavors

CAJUN SPICE BLEND

As close as you can get to New Orleans in a bottle! Regarding the dried sweet red chilies, see the index of this book. Simply combine all of

	CAJUN SPICE BLEND
2	Dried Sweet Red Chilies (stems removed)
2 t	Salt, Kosher (coarse)
1 1/2 t	Dark Brown Sugar, ideally Cassonade
1 t	Cayenne Pepper
1 t	Thyme, dried
3/4 t	Cumin Seeds
3/4 t	White Peppercorns
3/4 t	MSG (Accent flavor enhancer)
1/2 t	Garlic Powder
1/2 t	Onion Powder
1/2 t	Oregano, dried
1/2 t	Sage, dried
1/4 t	Black Peppercorns
1/4 t	Fennel Seeds

the ingredients in an electric spice mill. Store in a sealed jar for up to two months, but best when fresh. Use this in place of Emeril's *Essence*, too.

133

GARAM MASALA

Also known as Indian warming spices. While there is no such thing as British curry powder in India, Garam Masala is a spice blend that is commonly used throughout India. This is a Punjabi type of Garam Masala.

GARAM MASALA	
2 T	Coriander Seeds
1 1/2 T	Cumin Seeds
8 pods	Cardamom, green
1 t	Black Peppercorns
1/2 t	Cloves, whole (the spice - not garlic)
2.5cm (1")	Cinnamon stick
1	Bay Leaf
1/2 t	Nutmeg, ground
1/2 t	Ginger, ground
1/2 t	Crushed Red Chili Flakes
1/8 t	Nigella (Black Cumin Seeds)

Heat a skillet and toast the coriander, cumin, cardamom pods, peppercorns, cinnamon stick, bay leaf and cloves briefly until the cumin seeds darken slightly. Do not burn them! Transfer to a spice grinder along with the nutmeg, ginger and nigella. Grind to a powder and store in an airtight container for up to two months. Compare the aroma of this with a commercially bottle Garam Masala and you will never buy the manufactured product again. The smell of this is intense and rich, and that's the flavor it will impart to your cooking.

HOFBRAU MEAT SEASONING

Back in the 1950's and 1960's, the San Francisco Bay Area (where I grew up) was home to a unique type of restaurant called a Hofbrau. These were German-themed, taking their name from a type of beer garden in Munich. As the years went by, the owners gradually dropped things like head cheese and blood sausage from the menus, and focused on simple carved meats (especially roast beef), mashed potatoes and other comfort foods in an attempt to appeal to Americans and compete with the up and coming fast food chains. Their star attraction of roast beef had a unique flavor that people couldn't duplicate at home. I worked at one such place briefly. The secret turned out to mostly be green peppercorns, which were almost unheard of in America at the time. This blend works magic on roast beef, either before or after you cook it.

HOFBRAU SEASONING

2 t	Black Peppercorns, whole
2 t	Garlic Powder
1 1/2 t	Sea Salt
1 t	Green Peppercorns, dried
1 t	Sugar
1/2 t	Tarragon, dried
1/2 t	Marjoram, dried
1/2 t	MSG
1/4 t	Rosemary, dried
1/4 t	Cumin, ground

Grind all of the ingredients together in an electric spice mill. Don't grind into a fine powder, though. Leave a little texture. This also works brilliantly on French Dip sandwiches. A sprinkle on sliced roast beef or other meat is all it takes. Don't forget the German mustard, horseradish, dark rye bread, and potato salad to complete the experience.

TAJIK MEAT SEASONING

The cuisine from this part of the world is seldom seen elsewhere because the nation is small and sparsely populated, as well as being extremely poor. The cuisine is primarily Central Asian, but was influenced

TAJIK SEASONING

2 t	Black Peppercorns
1 1/2 t	Cumin Seeds
1 1/2 t	Salt
1 t	Anise Seeds
1 t	Mint, dried
1 t	Dill, dried
3/4 t	Chives, dried
1/2 t	Parsley, dried
1/8 t	Saffron
1 to 4	Dried Hot Red Chilies (see text below)

under Soviet rule. This is a very interesting spice blend that will bring a unique flavor to any dish, being especially good for lamb and vegetables. Hot dried red chilies are needed to complete this mixture, but I am not specifying the quantity because you need to be decide the heat independently from other flavors, and it will also depend on your taste.

Food preparation in Tajikistan.

SHARENA SOL

This is a traditional spice blend in Bulgaria. Every Bulgarian chef has their own favorite specific secret blend, but Sharena Sol invariably includes all of these ingredients in some proportion. One of the peculiar things about Russia is that up until recently, individual herbs and spices were difficult to find, and even then it was only the most basic seasonings. Yet there are dozens of spice blends available, mostly labeled for the intended purpose (shashlik seasoning, chicken seasoning, rice flavoring, etc.) The ingredients in these mixes are things that you can't buy individually. Russians purchase and use these mixtures without having any idea what it is they are using. Almost no one has ever heard of these ingredients, and they have no idea what they taste like individually. Several spice blends that are marketed are versions of Sharena Sol, which is natural because Bulgaria is a common vacation spot for Russians, and the food there is generally considered good. So it was a safe bet for spice manufacturers to copy this formula.

SHARENA SOL	
2 T	Summer Savory, dried (see note below)
1 T	Fenugreek, ground
1 T	Paprika, mild
1 1/2 t	Salt
1/2 t	Black Pepper, finely ground

Simply combine the ingredients. Note that there is some confusion about what is exactly meant by "summer savory" because there are different herbs in Bulgaria that are collected and marketed by the same name, and frequently the one used is actually a member of the thyme family (of which there are more than 200 different varieties, many with a distinctly different flavor from what thyme tastes like elsewhere). This is a good spice blend for eggs, especially.

Killer Cocktails!

As you probably know from my videos on YouTube, I am the author of *Cocktails of the South Pacific and Beyond*. The choice of what to drink with your food is almost as important as the food itself for total enjoyment. This is tragically overlooked by many people who have not yet experienced the sensory delight of a properly paired alcoholic drink with their food. This is especially the case for spicy foods, where the right cocktail can transform the single note of heat into a whole spectrum of tastes that only exist from this magical symbiotic relationship. The drinks presented here were all developed since the publication of my cocktail book. There are no duplicates.

BOMBAY THE HARD WAY

This is an especially interesting combination with chicken curry. The blend of gin with this Italian liqueur and cardamom has appeared on the menu of several cocktail bars in recent years, often under this name. Here is my take on this...

45ml (1.5oz)	Gin, Bombay or (better) Hendricks
30ml (1 oz)	Amaro Montenegro (an Italian liqueur)
15ml (1 tablespoon)	Lemon Juice, fresh
12ml (2.5 teaspoons)	Cardamom Solution (see following page)
5 drops	Maraschino Liqueur
curled strip	Orange Peel

Stir (don't shake) with ice and pour contents into a chilled glass.

CARDAMOM SOLUTION

60ml (2 oz)	Water
22g (3/4 oz)	Brown Sugar, or (better) Dark Muscavado
6 pods	Cardamom (green) - crushed in a mortar

Microwave for one minute. Stir and then cover with cling film and allow it to stand for an hour. Strain off the solids.

Y

KALINA

Especially well suited as a dessert drink after spicy food.

60ml (2 oz)	Italian Brandy or substitute Cognac
15ml (1/2 oz)	Vodka
15ml (1/2 oz)	Lemon Juice, fresh
12ml (2.5 teaspoons)	Maple Syrup
5ml (1 teaspoon)	Riga Black Balsam (Latvian bitter liqueur)
2.5ml (1/2 teaspoon)	Aperol (an Italian bitter orange liqueur)
2.5ml (1/2 teaspoon)	Maraschino Liqueur

Shake with ice and strain into a chilled glass with or without ice.

Y

LOST DUTCHMAN'S MIND

Gives the illusion of being a dark chocolate cocktail, even though the only actual chocolate is on the rim of the glass. Note that pomegranate molasses is not grenadine. Don't substitue them.

75ml (2.5oz)	Vodka, premium
15ml (1 tablespoon)	Pomegranate Molasses
15ml (1 tablespoon)	Sweet Italian Vermouth
5ml (1 teaspoon)	Cointreau
5ml (1 teaspoon)	Lime Juice, fresh
3-4 drops	Angostura bitters

Rub the rim of a martini glass with the lime and then coat with bittersweet cocoa powder. Shake with ice and strain into the glass.

ANGOSTURIA

This is an exotic taste with many layers of flavor. Refreshing on a hot summer day, but also nice after a late night coffee or dessert.

2 strips	Orange Peel (use a vegetable peeler)
15ml (1/2 oz)	Cognac, Hennessy *VSOP*
1 teaspoon	Dark Brown Sugar, preferably Muscovado

Muddle these ingredients in the bottom of the shaker, then add:

30ml (1 oz)	Gin, Beefeater
15ml (1/2 oz)	Benedictine
7.5ml (3/4 oz)	Lemon Juice, fresh

Shake with ice and strain into a chilled goblet over cracked ice. Sprinkle over the top:

5-8 drops	Angostura bitters

Serve with a small diameter straw.

SCREAMING BLUE PINES

Incorporating two of the most famous liquors from Austria, this is a powerhouse cocktail that will keep you coming back for more...after you wake up from the first one, that is! Zirben is made from an unusual blue pine cone that grows high in the Alps. If you have tasted it straight, you know why it is an acquired taste favored mostly by local Austrians - it has an unpleasant aftertaste that is reminiscent of furniture polish. However, with a little mixological magic, it conjures images of forest berries and Alpine ski trips from dreams that you forgot you ever had. Delicious, but not for the faint of heart. Substitute Stroh 60 to make it a bit less potent.

45ml (1.5 oz)	Zirben Likör
30ml (1 oz)	Stroh 80 (Austrian high-proof spiced rum)
22ml (3/4 oz)	Creme de Cassis, Bols
15ml (1/2 oz)	Lime Juice, fresh
dash (about 1/4 t)	Sweet Italian Vermouth, Martini & Rossi

Shake with ice and strain into a chilled glass with or without ice.

REPOSE

Winner of several contests including 2011 *Cocktail of the Year* in Los Angeles - and one of my own personal favorites for a long time now, I am especially proud of this monstrosity.

30ml (1 oz)	Gin, Tanqueray Ten
30ml (1 oz)	Dark Rum, Bacardi Black
30ml (1 oz)	Lingonberry Liqueur, Laponnia
	or Lingonberry Nastoyka (see next recipe)
30ml (1 oz)	Vodka
15ml (1 tablespoon)	Triple Sec Royal Orange, or Cointreau
7.5ml (1/4 oz)	Sweet Italian Vermouth, Martini & Rossi
large strip	Grapefruit Zest, cut decoratively
1 teaspoon	Apricot Jam

Stir the ingredients together with a spoon for 20-30 seconds, then add ice and shake gently. Be careful not to destroy the grapefruit zest garnish in the shaker. Strain into a highball glass containing 3 ice cubes, fishing out the piece of grapefruit zest in the process. Squeeze:

1/2	Lime

...over the drink, then drop the lime shell on top of the ice cubes. Drape the grapefruit zest over the top of the lime shell to support its weight. Add a straw and settle in for some deep thoughts.

LINGONBERRY NASTOYKA

This may be served on the rocks, or used in mixing cocktails.

150g (5.3 oz)	Lingonberries, frozen
200g (7 oz)	Sugar
250ml (8.8 oz)	Vodka

Combine in a sauce pan and bring to a gentle simmer. Pour into a covered container and allow to stand at room temperature for 24 hours. Strain off the lingonberries, but do not press down on them. You can use the alcohol-cured lingonberries in cooking (especially desserts) and if you refrigerate them, they keep for many months.

MONSTER IN THE ROOT CELLAR

It isn't every day that you see a cocktail that incorporates root beer as a mixer, but this downright weirdly spectacular concoction comes together as surprisingly uplifting. Pickled burdock is available in Japanese markets. It is usually dyed orange and looks like a carrot, but tastes nothing like a carrot.

45ml (1 1/2 oz)	Vodka
30ml (1 oz)	Becharovka (Czech herbal liqueur)
30ml (1 oz)	Root Beer, Francis Hartridge
15ml (1/2 oz)	Lime Juice, fresh
8-10 drops	Scrappy's Orleans Bitters

Combine ingredients in shaker with ice. Pour out into a frozen rocks glass and garnish with:

1 each	Fennel frond
1 piece	Pickled Burdock, rinsed (see note above)
1 center slice	Watermelon Radish with green stem intact

CITRUS GIN FIZZ

This is a version of the classic Ramos Gin Fizz, only better (in my opinion). Have a listen to the Tiger Lillies song *Gin* while you're at it.

60ml (2 oz)	Gin, Tanqueray
22-30 ml (3/4 - 1 oz)	Cointreau (see note below)
20ml (2/3 oz)	Cream
15ml (1/2 oz)	Lime Juice, fresh
15ml (1/2 oz)	Lemon Juice, fresh
10ml (2 t)	Wild Rose Hips Syrup
1/2	Egg White

Wash the outside of the egg with warm soapy water before you crack it to avoid salmonella. Use the smaller measure of Cointreau stated for a dry cocktail, and the larger measure for a sweeter version. Combine all ingredients in shaker with ice cubes. Wrap the shaker in a bar towel and shake vigorously for 2 minutes. Strain into a chilled highball glass. Add an orange slice and a straw.

BRONZE BUMPER

Pull up to the bumper, baby! Inspired by a cocktail served at a luxury resort in Aquiraz, Brazil. *Everyone* asks for a second round! The cognac version is different, but also extremely good.

45ml (1 1/2 oz) Cachaça, or Cognac (see note above)
45ml (1 1/2 oz) Amaretto
45ml (1 1/2 oz) Pineapple Juice
22ml (3/4 oz) Lemon Juice, fresh
1 to 1 1/2 t   Fernet-Branca (Italian bitter liqueur)
2.5ml (1/2 t) Orgeat syrup

Combine all ingredients in shaker with ice cubes. Shake for about 10 seconds to create froth. Pour the entire contents including the ice into a chilled decorative crystal goblet. Add 2-3 <u>grapefruit</u> <u>curls</u> and stir them through to perfume the drink. Add a narrow straw.

FLYING PINK UNICORN

It's a girly drink by name and by color, but make sure you have a ride home before starting in on these. Hint: this unicorn isn't going anywhere near your house.

60ml (2 oz)	Vodka
30ml (1 oz)	White Overproof Rum, J Wray and Nephew
30ml (1 oz)	Cranberry Juice
15ml (1/2 oz)	Creme de Noyaux, Bols
10ml (2 t)	Lime Juice, fresh
1/2 teaspoon	Maraschino Liqueur

Combine all ingredients in shaker with ice cubes. Strain into a glass rimmed with pink sugar. Add a cherry. The decorative blown glass unicorn swizzle sticks that we use are available online.

144

KING OF DIAMONDS

This is a based on a Kir Royale, but dryer, stronger, and much more interesting. This is my cocktail of choice on New Years Eve. Be sure not to confuse this Black Balsam with the original and more common bitter liqueur in the brown bottle (both are from the same company in Latvia). *Currant* has a black bottle with a purple label. One popular choice for the sparkling wine is Henkell Trocken Rosé.

45ml (1 1/2 oz)	Moldovan Brandy, or substitute cognac
30ml (1 oz)	Riga Black Balsam *Currant* (see note above)
15ml (1/2 oz)	Vodka
15ml (1/2 oz)	Sweet Italian Vermouth, Martini & Rossi
1 teaspoon	Lemon Juice, fresh

Combine all ingredients in shaker with ice cubes. Shake, and then add *approximately*:

30ml (1 oz)	Brut Champagne or Sparkling Wine

Strain into a champagne glass over a slice of tinned peach as a garnish. Add a sprig of mint, if desired.

MOUNTAIN JEW

Not to be confused with the soft drink of a similar name. Sabra is an Israeli bittersweet chocolate and orange liqueur that may be difficult to find. You can make a good version of this by substituting the Sabra for equal parts Godiva Dark Chocolate Liqueur (or dark Creme de Cacao) and Cointreau.

30ml (1 oz)	Sabra (see note above)
30ml (1 oz)	Vodka
15ml (1/2 oz)	Lime Juice, fresh
4-6 drops	Lime bitters, or (quite different) Orange bitters

Combine all ingredients in shaker with ice cubes. Empty contents into a highball glass or goblet. Top with a blast of seltzer water and add a straw.

NOTES

NOTES

Shopping Lists & Notes

One of the most frequent requests that I receive is for a printable list of ingredients for the recipes online. This appendix contains a shopping list for virtually every recipe that has been put up on YouTube through December, 2014 - and more.

Note: in some cases basic supplies such as vegetable oil, butter, flour, water, sugar, salt and pepper have not been copied into the shopping list here in order to leave room for the extra notes that I have added for each recipe—tips and variations that were not covered in the videos. Be sure to consult the video for the full ingredient list so you don't leave anything out.

www.youtube.com/user/cookinginrussia

On this site you will see a short video explaining how to find my other video recipes, which begin on the next page of this book.

Chicken Cacciatore

6 Chicken Thighs, LARGE & bone-in (just under 2 pounds)

120 g (4 oz) Mushrooms, ideally Porcini

2 T. Butter + 30 ml (1 oz) Cognac if button mushrooms used)

100 g (3 1/2 oz) Tomato Sauce, Italian boxed

120 g (4 oz) Onion, diced medium

100 g (3 1/2 oz) Celery Root, cut in strips (Celeriac)

100 g (3 1/2 oz) Red Bell Pepper, cubed

100 g (3 1/2 oz) Carrot, diced medium

60 g (2 oz) Fennel, diced medium

100 g (3 1/2 oz) Tomato, diced (fresh in season, else canned)

8 Garlic cloves, whole

1 1/2 t. Black Peppercorns, freshly cracked

Dried Rosemary, Oregano, and Basil

350 ml (1 1/2 C) Red Wine - ideally Barolo

1 Chili Pepper, minced. Ideally Hungarian Yellow, but Fresno is okay

2 t. Sugar

1 T. Parsley, minced fresh

Salt

ADDITIONAL NOTES

This video continues to be one of my most popular and highly rated recipes, despite there being hundreds of recipes for this dish online. The reason is that this dish is absolutely delicious when it is properly made, and all modesty aside, this is the best recipe anywhere. If you have tried Cacciatore before and thought you didn't like it, try this recipe.

The only secret is the quality of the wine you use. Don't go cheap.

Sicilian Chicken Agridulce

1 Whole "Fryer" Chicken, cut in 10 pieces (back not used)

300 g (10 oz) Fennel bulb(s), sliced into broad strips

300 g (10 oz) Onion, coarsely cubed

12 Caperberries, rinsed (not capers)

6 Garlic cloves, sliced

Olive Oil (extra virgin)

Sugar

White Wine

Red Wine Vinegar

Salt and Pepper

ADDITIONAL NOTES

This is a simple Sicilian dish that has been a classic for a very long time. You can add in a little orange zest, lemon zest, orange juice, and lemon juice, as is often done in Sicily, but then you will need to adjust the amount of sugar and red wine vinegar. Don't go overboard, or it will start to taste like a Chinese sweet and sour dish. A little citrus gives it a nice touch, but finding the balance will take some skill in tasting, which is why I avoided getting into that in the video.

Chinese/Korean
Braised Shortribs

750 g (1 3/4 lb) Beef Short Ribs

250 ml (1 cup) Soy Sauce

250 ml (1 cup) Shao Xing or Sherry, medium dry

25 g (just under 1 oz) Ginger

25 g (just under 1 oz) Garlic

50 g (just under 2 oz) Carrot

50 g (just under 2 oz) Scallions

1 T Liquid Smoke

2-3 T Brown Sugar

1 Red Chili, seeded

2 T Chinese Five Spice Powder (see below)

1 t Corn Starch

ADDITIONAL NOTES

Chinese Five Spice is a blend of equal parts of Cloves, Sichuan Peppercorns, Cinnamon Stick, Fennel Seeds and Star Anise. Making your own will ensure it is fresh. Once these spices have been ground up, they do not keep very long.

Koreans normally add sliced pear to this in place of the brown sugar. The results are slightly better, but in a commercial restaurant kitchen, brown sugar is much less expensive than pears.

Sicilian Stuffed Eggplant

2 Eggplants, not too large

3 T Olive Oil + more for baking the eggplant

60 g (2 oz) Fennel bulb, sliced thin

200 g (7 oz) Onion, chopped medium fine

1 Red Chili Pepper, seeded and diced

1 t Sugar

2 T Pine Nuts (also known as pignolia)

15 g (1/2 oz) Garlic cloves

20 g (3/4 oz) Golden Raisins

60 ml (2 oz) White Wine, dry

2 Anchovy filets, soaked in milk (optional)

15-20 g (1/2 oz+) Parmigiano Reggiano cheese

15 g (1/2 oz) Breadcrumbs, dry

1 Egg Yolk

1 t Orange Zest

Red Chili Flakes & Good Olive Oil to finish

ADDITIONAL NOTES

This was one of the first recipes that I put up, and one that I regret not having provided more details, or photographing it better, but YouTube doesn't allow for edits to videos after they are posted. There are many variations of this recipe that are popular and delicious. It is more traditional to prick them with a fork all over and then boil the eggplants in salted water to soften them as a first step. This will leave them tasting more neutral. When you roast them, as I do here, the eggplant flavor is intensified. It is a matter of personal taste. If you like the nuttiness of the eggplant flavor, this method is superior.

Braised Pork in Pastry
(Porc Braisé en Pâtisserie)

1 kg (2 1/4 lb) Pork Roast, trimmed as shown

8 strips Smoked Bacon (2 at first, 6 more later)

Olive Oil

500 ml (2 cups) Chicken Stock, low salt

1 Onion, coarsely cubed

1 Carrot, diced medium

45 ml (1 1/2 oz) Balsamic Vinegar

2 Bay Leaves

6 Garlic cloves

2 T. Celery Leaves

Puff Pastry Sheet

Coarse Salt and Peppercorns

Mustard (mix with mayonnaise if mustard is strong)

1 Egg Yolk

ADDITIONAL NOTES

The success of this dish will depend almost entirely on the nature of the pork you are using. If you have very lean pork (as is often the problem in American pork), the result will be dry and chewy. If you have very fatty pork (as is frequently the problem in eastern Europe), the meat will leak juices into the pastry from the inside, resulting in a soggy dough that won't cook through. The perfect result can only be obtained with pork that is evenly and lightly marbled with no heavy streaks of solid fat, and no completely lean regions that will be dry. This sort of pork is relatively easy to find in France, Italy and Spain, but hard to come by in most other countries.

Amazing Faux BBQ Chicken

900 g (2 lbs) Chicken, thighs and legs are best

200 g (7 oz) Tomato Sauce (Italian pasata)

170 g (6 oz) Onion (or part onion and part shallot)

50 g (2 1/2 oz) Red Bell Pepper

30 g (1 oz) Garlic cloves

1 T (15 g, or 1/2 oz) Liquid Smoke

1 Star Anise

6 Cloves, whole (the spice)

1 t Thyme, dried

2 Bay Leaves

1 t Black Peppercorns

100 g Apple Cider Vinegar

50 g Brown Sugar

2 T Vegetable Oil

15 g (1 T) Honey

1/2 t Mustard, strong

2-3 T Flour

ADDITIONAL NOTES

As just about everyone who has tried this recipe has said, this video deserved a lot more attention than it received. This was put up on YouTube at a time when I had very few subscribers and has since been buried under a hundred more recent videos, but if you like BBQ chicken, I encourage you to try this.

Eggs Florentine (Belgian Version)

15 g (1/2 oz) Butter

1 T Flour

1 t Shallot, minced

30 g (1 oz) Parmesan Cheese

100 ml (3 1/2 oz) Half & Half (half cream and half milk)

15 g (1/2 oz) Spinach, coarsely chopped

10 ml (1/3 oz) Lemon Juice

1/4 t Dry Mustard (such as Coleman's)

Nutmeg

Salt and White Pepper

Slices of a Baguette

Olive Oil

1 Egg, whole - brought to room temperature

ADDITIONAL NOTES

Many years ago on a trip to Brussels, there was a restaurant near my hotel where I ate breakfast every morning. After telling the waitress how much I enjoyed this particular dish, one thing led to another, and the next thing I knew, I was in the kitchen with the French chef explaining to me how to make it, step by step - even writing the recipe down for me as he went along. Not that it is especially complicated, but the balance of flavors is very nice - even if it is rather obviously 1970's European cuisine.

You should also consider addling strips of prosciutto with this, and don't forget to taste it and adjust the salt.

Stuffed Russian Peppers

150 g (5 oz) Potatoes, peeled
50 g (1 3/4 oz) Carrot, peeled
30 g (1 oz) Shallot
75 g (2 1/2 oz) Smoked Cheese
2 T Ricotta
75-90 g (2 1/2 - 3 oz) Sausage
3 T Celery Leaves, chopped coarsely
1-2 Garlic cloves
5-6 Small Peppers for stuffing
Salt and Pepper
Red Wine Vinegar
Chili Oil (you can use the same one as for Indian food - see index)
Sour Cream

ADDITIONAL NOTES

Wherever there are peppers, there are local recipes for stuffing them. The success of this recipe will be determined by your choice of ingredients. Try smoked edam for the cheese and instead of a single type of sausage, make it a mixture of cooked ham, bacon and sausage.

Stuffed Pork Chops

2 Pork Chops, previously brined

60g (2 oz) Chanterelle Mushrooms

30g (1 oz) Red Onion or Shallots, chopped fine

2 T Parmesan cheese, finely grated

1 T Lemon juice, fresh

2 cloves Garlic, finely sliced

1/2 t Tarragon, dried

3/4 t Dill, dried

1/2 t Poulet Glace (concentrated chicken stock)

2-3 T Bread crumbs, dry

1/2 t Mustard, prepared

Butter, Vegetable Oil, Salt and Pepper

Additional Red Onion or Shallot for baking

ADDITIONAL NOTES

This recipe is best with dried herbs, not fresh. I know this seems counterintuitive at a time when every chef is extolling the virtues of fresh ingredients, but dried tarragon and dill are quite different in their flavor profile from when they are fresh. I explain this in more detail in my video, *#2 ORGANIC CHEMISTRY IN COOKING - Dried vs Fresh Herbs*.

For the Poulet Glace, you can make your own using the same method that I use for making the Rabbit Glace in my video, *1 RABBIT AS A FOUR COURSE MEAL FOR 2,* or you can also use some of a Knorr Chicken Stock gel pack (not the dry cube). The difference will not be very noticeable here because it is such a small amount.

Chicken with Artichokes and Chanterelles

2 Artichokes

6-8 Chicken Thighs

150g (5 oz) Chanterelles (or other mushrooms)

200g (7oz) Red Onion, diced

60g (2oz) Celery, diced

6-8 Garlic cloves, whole

1 t Oregano, dried

3/4 t White Pepper, fresh ground

1/2 t Parsley, dried

1 t Brown Sugar

100ml (3 1/2 oz) White Wine, dry

250ml (8 1/2 oz) Chicken Stock

Lemons for juice

Flour

Red Chili Flakes (optional)

ADDITIONAL NOTES

Here is another example of an early video that I put up before I had very many subscribers, and so it never really got the attention that it deserves. This is a delicious and beautiful dish. The only problem that people have with it is the cooking of the artichokes. You have to use a relatively low heat and be patient. Test them with a toothpick if you aren't sure when they are done. Artichokes are most often boiled, but really that is a terrible way of cooking them, because most of the flavor leaches out into the surrounding water. Artichokes are best fried, or even microwaved. Yes - microwaved! It is one of the few items that cooks beautifully in a microwave. I may produce a video on how to do this in the upcoming months. Feel free to remind me!

Shrimp Saag (Indian Prawn Curry)

180g (6 oz) Large Shrimp, raw with shell-on

350ml (12 oz) Fish Stock (or use Knorr Fish Stock - see video)

50g (just under 2 oz) Red Onion

35g (1 1/4 oz) Garlic cloves

30g (1 oz) Red Bell Pepper

1 1/2 T Ginger, grated

1/4 Red Chili Pepper

75g (2 1/2 oz) Tomato Sauce (packaged)

150g (5 1/2 oz) Potato, cut in 1/2 inch dice

1 T Brown Sugar

2 to 3 T Cilantro, chopped

1/2 t Paprika

2 Bay Leaves

125g (4 1/2 oz) fresh baby Spinach, washed well

60g (2 oz) Kefir, buttermilk or plain yogurt

30g (1 oz) Butter

Salt and Pepper

Lemon

ADDITIONAL NOTES

The use of shrimp stock instead of ordinary fish stock will improve this dish. The way to have shrimp stock on hand is to always purchase whole shrimp, then save the shells and tails in a plastic box in your freezer as you cook them. When you have enough, you can make a shrimp stock with them. You can bolster the strength of the shrimp stock with inexpensive frozen bay shrimp.

Beef Bourguignon

600g (20 oz) Beef Round or Sirloin Roast (weight after trimming)

1/2 bottle good red wine, ideally Côtes du Rhone

2 cloves Garlic

2 Bay Leaves

125g (4 oz) Bacon (cut thick)

125g (4 oz) Onion, diced medium

60g (2 oz) Tomato Purée (pasata)

2 medium Carrots

150g Cipolini Onions, or other small variety

150g Mushrooms

250ml (8 oz) Beef Stock

30ml (1 oz) Cognac

3/4 t Thyme, dried (or a few sprigs of the fresh herb)

ADDITIONAL NOTES

There are two keys to the success of this dish. The first is not to shortchange the braise time. This applies to all braised dishes, but especially this one. Second, the selection of meat. Feel the meat with your fingers. If you have never tried doing this before with a group of different cuts of meat, you will likely be surprised at how obvious it becomes as to which pieces will be tough. Butchers know this trick well, and in the course of their work, they often set aside remarkably soft pieces they come across for themselves to take home. Every cow is a little different. Of course the other factor is fat striation. You want some. Ultra lean beef is ultra tough beef. If you are really afraid of fat, then expect tough beef. However, that doesn't mean it needs to look like Kobe beef to be tender, either. You don't want huge chunks of fat, nor do you want red meat without a speck of white. Aim for well striated meat that is soft to the touch.

Chicken Korma

2 lbs (900g) Chicken Thighs, bone-in

1 C (250ml) Chicken Stock

1 oz (30g) Cashew Nuts

Onions

Ginger

Garlic

Cilantro, fresh

Lemon

3 1/2 oz (100g) Yoghurt, plain and NOT non-fat

Brown Sugar

Butter and Vegetable Oil (or use Ghee)

1/2 t Mustard Seeds

2 t Coriander Seeds

1 t Black Peppercorns

1 t Cloves

3 t Cumin Seeds

1 t Fennel Seeds

1 t Cinnamon (ground)

2 t Turmeric

1 1/2 t Cayenne Pepper

2 Bay Leaves

1/4 t Asafoetida

ADDITIONAL NOTES

Note that the quantity of spices shown are the total amounts used.
This remains one of my most popular videos. The reason is that
there are a great many Chicken Korma recipes online, but nearly all
of them are quite terrible. This delivers absolutely great flavor.

Naan (Indian Bread)

2-3 C Flour

1 C (250ml) Milk, ideally 3.5% fat

1 t Sugar

1 package Yeast

1 Egg

6 cloves Garlic

1/4 C (100ml) Vegetable Oil

1/2 t Liquid Smoke (optional)

Salt

ADDITIONAL NOTES

Use fresh yeast, if at all possible. There is a reason that professional bakers and pizzerias use fresh instead of freeze dried yeast - the flavor and texture are better.

Don't be afraid of a little bit of burning, but if you are getting large patches of black, then reduce your heat.

Madras Cauliflower Curry (Electric Lotus)

650g (1 1/2 lb) Cauliflower, trimmed

4 cloves Garlic

1 T Ginger, grated

1/2 Tomato, or 30g (1 oz) Tomato Paste (actually better in this case)

75g (2 1/2 oz) Vegetable Oil, or Ghee

125g (4 oz) Yogurt, plain

Basil (dried)

Cilantro, fresh

Also the following spices:

Turmeric, Cumin Seeds, Allspice, Black Peppercorns, Mustard Seeds, Fenugreek (ground), Cayenne Pepper

ADDITIONAL NOTES

The fan assist feature in the oven is important to this dish, because it will blow out the moisture exuded by the cauliflower during the first stage of cooking. If you do not have this in your oven, then double the first stage of cooking time (before you put the lid on it).

Georgian Khachapuri "Quiche"

Dough from the Naan recipe (see separate video and index)
45g (1 1/2 oz) Kostromskaya (or substitute Jack)
45g (1 1/2 oz) Mozzarella
45g (1 12 oz) Gruyere, or Swiss Cheese
30g (1 oz) Parmesan
Onion
Flour
Butter

ADDITIONAL NOTES
You can also add spinach and/or cooked bacon inside.

Russian Style Spatchcock BBQ Chicken

1 or 2 Roasting Chickens, whole

1/2 Red Onion, peeled and sliced

1/2 Carrot, peeled and sliced

1 Tomato, diced

3 cloves Garlic, coarsely chopped

Coriander Seeds

Mixed Peppercorns

Cayenne Pepper

Cider Vinegar

Liquid Smoke (ideally mesquite)

ADDITIONAL NOTES

The chicken is extremely tender after being cooked in this way, so you are advised to use a BBQ grill basket for the second stage of cooking over coals, as shown in the image below...

Butter Chicken (Indian Tikka Masala)

Chicken Thighs, boneless and skinless

1 1/2 t. Ground Dry Ginger

1 t. EACH Paprika, Cayenne, Cumin Seeds, Coriander Seeds, Ground Cinnamon, Garlic Powder, Sugar, Salt

1/2 t. EACH Black Peppercorns, Ground Fenugreek (Methi)

4 Whole Cloves (the spice - not garlic)

2 Brown Cardamon Pods, whole

120 g (4 oz) Yogurt

1 T. Lemon Juice

Red Food Coloring (optional)

90g (3oz) Clarified Butter (Ghee)

2 T Coconut, dry and unsweetened

1 T Green Cardamon Pods, whole (less if they are very fresh)

1 1/2 t. Nutmeg

1 Bay Leaf

6 Allspice Berries, whole

22g (3/4oz) Garlic, cut in large pieces

700g (1 1/2 lbs) Tomatoes (must be ripe)

2 Green Chili Peppers (Serrano)

22g (3/4oz) Ginger

60g (2oz) Onion

1 t Paprika

1 1/2 Cups Chicken Stock (or water)

45ml (1 1/2 oz) Cream

2-3 T Yogurt

1/2 t Curry Powder

1/2 t Liquid Smoke

Beef Stroganoff

2.2kg (3lbs) Beef, bone-in shoulder, as shown

Black Peppercorns, Garlic Powder

1 Star Anise pod

1 Onion, medium

120g (4oz) Tomatoes, pureéd (pasata)

180ml (6oz) Red Wine, dry (total amount used)

45ml (1 1/2oz) Cognac or Brandy

180g (6oz) Mushrooms, quartered

Fresh Dill and Parsley, and 2 Bay Leaves

Paprika

45g (1 1/2oz) Butter

PASTA

200g (6 2/3oz) Flour

2 Eggs, whole

30-40g (just over 1 oz) Sour Cream (optional - see note below)

Fresh Parsley

ADDITIONAL NOTES

If you are not an expert at making pasta, replace the sour cream with a little cold water. Sour cream makes it more difficult to work with, although the results are better if you can handle it.

This dish can be prepared faster and with excellent results in another manner, but that requires a more expensive cut of beef. The advantage of this method is that it is economical, which is important for a restaurant, certainly. If you want to see another way of making this using ribeye steak (entrecôte), leave feedback or send me email. If enough people request it, I'll make it a video.

"Polynesian" Chicken & Potato Curry

1 1/2 t Allspice

1 1/2 t Cumin Seeds

3/4 t Black Peppercorns

3/4 t Coriander Seeds

3/4 t Mustard Seeds

6 Green Cardamom pods, whole

30g (1 oz) Butter, melted (preferably clarified, or use ghee)

1 Green Serrano Chili, chopped coarsely

45g (1 1/2 oz) Onion, coarsely chopped

90g (3 oz) Tomatoes, fresh

1/2 t Turmeric

15 g (1/2 oz) Ginger, grated

15 g (1/2 oz) Garlic, chopped coarsely

2 t Salt

1 t Sugar

1 T Lime Juice

5-8 Chicken Thighs, boneless, skinless

1 Onion, medium

30g (1 oz) Vegetable Oil

200g (7 oz) Coconut Milk, unsweetened

200g (7 oz) Chicken Stock

2 Potatoes, cut in large pieces

1 t Thai Fish Sauce (Nam Pla)

1 t Basil, dried

Cilantro for garnish

This is another recipe that deserved more attention than it has
received. If you like Thai or Indian food, you will certainly enjoy this!

Real Vindaloo (Portuguese & Goan Indian Curry)

2 T Vegetable Oil, or Ghee

180g (6 oz) Onion, sliced

2 t Black Peppercorns

1 t Black Mustard Seeds (or brown)

3/4 t Allspice, whole

3/4 t Fenugreek, whole

1 Tomato, core removed then cut in pieces

2 t Salt

530ml (2 1/4 C) Dry Red Wine

25g (~3/4 oz) Garlic, cloves cut in thirds

1-2 Bay Leaves (ideally fresh)

2 T Vegetable Oil, or Ghee

600-800g (1 1/2 lbs) Beef cut in large cubes

  * You can use also use pork - but not too lean!

2 t Cumin, ground

1 t Cardamom, ground

1-6 Red Chilies, dried - preferably Kashmari

3 T Red Wine Vinegar

2 cloves Garlic

1 1/2 t Dark Brown Sugar

Sliced Onion & Chili Peppers for garnish

ADDITIONAL NOTES

This improves after a few days in refrigeration, but make it spicier than you want the final dish to be if you are going to store it because the heat diminishes a great deal over time.

Tender and Moist Herbed Chicken Breasts

Chicken Cap(s) - about 800g (2 lb) each

Butter

Garlic (one clove per cap)

Coarse Salt

Dry Herbs (2 teaspoons per cap)

I suggest thyme, tarragon and chives, which is classic

Fresh ground Black Pepper

Paprika

Lemon Slices

Onion Slices

ADDITIONAL NOTES

The size of the cap (also called a crown) is important for the cooking time. If you are using smaller chickens, then the time will be shorter, of course. Your goal is to just cook the chicken without drying it out.

French Chicken with Mushrooms
or Chicken a La King

6 Large Mushrooms

60ml (2 oz) Sherry, Spanish Oloroso variety

1/2 Onion (carrot and celery are optional)

120ml (4 oz) Cream

Butter, Olive Oil, Flour, Salt

2 Eggs (yolks only)

Paprika and White Pepper, ground

White Truffle Oil, or (better) White Truffle shavings

45g (1 1/2 oz) Peas, frozen

30g (1 oz) Red Bell Pepper, cooked

　* Pimento would be better, though

Cooked noodles, such as fettuccine

ADDITIONAL NOTES

In place of the sherry, you can substitute Sauternes for even better results. The magic of this dish is the white truffle. You should also be aware that "white truffle oil" is often just olive oil with an artificial chemical flavoring added to it, and it has no actual truffle in it. The price you pay for the oil is usually a good indication of what you are getting. Truffle oil made with actual truffles will sometimes have pieces of truffle visible in the oil as proof that it isn't a chemical fake. Although a bottle of real truffle oil (from France or Italy) is typically 5 to 10 times as much as the industrial fake, you can keep it in the refrigerator for many months, and a few drops will vastly improve a a wide variety of dishes.

Magic No-Kneading French Bread

500g (17.6 ounces) Flour (AP or high-gluten)

1 T (1 package dried) Yeast

2 t Salt

300ml (10.6 ounces) Warm Water

100ml (3.5 ounces) Hoegaarden Ale

ADDITIONAL NOTES

As always, fresh yeast will provide even better results.

While you can substitute other "live" beers (those that have living yeast cultures in the bottle), you will get reliably good results from Hoegaarden, which is now available almost everywhere in the world.

Oaxacan Pork Mole

About 12 chilies of various types. I used 8 sweet chilies (as described in the first part of this book) and 4 hot serrano chilies, both red and green. This was because of the limited choice in chilies that I have here. Use more variety if you can.

1 T bacon grease or oil

cinnamon stick

2 star anise

1 T cumin seeds

1/2 t cloves (whole)

1 t allspice (whole)

30g / 1oz golden raisins

60g / 2oz almonds

2 T sesame seeds

1 1/2 T cocoa powder

1 T dark brown sugar

120g / 4oz tomato purée (pasata)

juice of 1 lime

3 cloves garlic

500ml / 2 cups chicken stock

1 1/2 t salt

about 30g / 1oz of stale bread cut into cubes

1 t liquid mesquite smoke (optional - see video).

900g/2lb pork (with some fat on it -- NOT lean)

cumin (dry powder)

cilantro

lime and sesame seeds to garnish

French Bistro Indoor Grilled Shrimp

200g (7 oz) Frozen Raw Large Shrimp, shell-on
400ml (14 oz) Water
1 Bay Leaf, 1/4 to 1/2 t Garlic Powder
Lemon Juice, fresh
Black Pepper, freshly ground

EITHER::
1 Knorr Shrimp Boullion Cube plus 1 1/2 t Salt
OR
3 t. Salt (not nearly as good)

ADDITIONAL NOTES
The word "bistro" is actually Russian, and it means to hurry. The word was picked up by the French when Napoleon invaded.

Moldavian Braised Vegetable Sauce

750g (26 1/2 oz) Tomatoes, fresh

200g (7 oz) Celery Root, also known as celeriac

200g (7 oz) Onion

90g (3 oz) Red Bell Pepper

1 Chili Pepper, small red

4 Garlic cloves

22g (3/4 oz) Parsley, fresh flat-leaf

Paprika

Olive Oil

250g (8 3/4 oz) Tomato Sauce (boxed tomato purée)

1/4 C of Basil, fresh

120mL (4 oz) Red Wine, dry and strong

30ml (1 oz) Cognac, preferably from Moldova

Sugar

Salt

ADDITIONAL NOTES

Moldavian cognac is a tremendous bargain. The flavor is much better than inexpensive French and Armenian cognacs, especially when it comes to cooking.

Moldavian Eggplant Parmesan

Moldavian Braised Vegetable Sauce (see separate video)

1-2 Eggplants - large

8 Garlic cloves

180g (6 oz) Flour

1 t. Marjoram, dried (optional)

Parmesan Cheese

Mozzarella

Sour Cream (*not mentioned in the video* - optional between layers)

ADDITIONAL NOTES

These can be made more decorative by peeling away stripes from the skin of the eggplant before slicing it (instead of completely peeling it). Then stack up the eggplant slices so that the black and white edges form a contrasting pattern around the outside. You can use a bamboo skewer to hold a tall stack together while it cooks. Once the cheese has melted you can remove the skewer and it will remain secure, of course. Top with chives or deep fried scallions.

Best Quality Brown Stock

2kg (4 1/2 lbs) Beef bones (see video)

1kg (2 1/4 lbs) Beef shoulder, bone-in

2 Onions (each used at different times)

2 Carrots (each used at different times)

300g Celery or Celery Root (used in two places)

Bunch of assorted herbs (parsley, thyme, dill, etc.)

2 Bay Leaves

2 Garlic cloves

3 T. Vermouth

Black Pepper, Garlic Powder, Thyme, Cloves

Butter

ADDITIONAL NOTES

Note that this is not the same thing as Veal Stock, which is neutral in flavor and can be used with almost any meat, fish or seafood. This stock has a pronounced beef flavor, and is only suitable in recipes for beef and veal.

You can scale this recipe up without it changing the cooking time, as long as you are counting the time from when it comes to a simmer (obviously 20 liters of stock will take a lot longer to heat up than 4 liters, for example - but I'm not counting the warm up time).

Classic French Onion Soup

750g (26 oz) Beef Stock

1.2kg (2.6 lbs) Yellow Onions

2 Bay Leaves

1 Garlic clove

Sherry Wine, dry -- not sweet

Balsamic Vinegar, good quality

Thyme (ideally fresh, but dried is okay)

Gruyere Cheese and Bread for croutons

Butter, Olive Oil, Salt, Pepper

ADDITIONAL NOTES

When I say good quality balsamic vinegar, I am not referring to the very expensive aged *Aceto Balsamico Tradizionale*. I just mean not to use a cheap supermarket brand, because those have synthetic flavorings in them that will leave a foul aftertaste on the palate.

The photo that I show at the end of this video is how Gordon Ramsay serves this dish. The photo was supplied to me by a friend who is one of the cooks at his Las Vegas restaurant. The more usual way of melting cheese over the top of the entire bowl is simple enough that I didn't think anyone needed directions for that, but I have received email from people asking. You simply add grated cheese and flash it under the salamander (or broiler) until it melts and begins to caramelize to your satisfaction. I would go back and add this as a segment to the end of the video, but YouTube does not allow for modifying videos once they are posted. The only option is removing it completely and uploading a new one, but then the people who had marked this one as a "favorite" would see a message showing the video has been deleted. This same sort of problem has occurred on several other videos I have posted. I would like to go back and add more to the video, but I can't.

Finnish Lihapullat
(Reindeer Meatballs)

180g (6oz) Reindeer meat - or substitute with other lean meat

45g (1 1/2 oz) Butter, cut in cubes and frozen solid

30g (1 oz) Breadcrumbs

30ml (1 oz) Cream

22g (3/4 oz) Shallot, finely minced

1 Egg Yolk

White Peppercorns

Allspice

Juniper Berries (dried)

FOR FORMAL PRESENTATION

180g (6oz) Potatoes, boiled until soft and cooled

1 T Sour Cream

1 Egg Yolk

Carrots, cut as shown later in the video

Lingonberries cooked with sugar and water (frozen is okay)

Mushrooms cooked in butter (preferably Chanterelles)

ADDITIONAL NOTES

I realize that many people have a revulsion to eating unfamiliar meats, especially when the animal is cute (*e.g.* bunnies), weird (*e.g.* ostriches), scary (*e.g.* snakes, insects), a cultural icon (*e.g.* horses), reminiscent of roadkill (*e.g.* raccoon), is strong smelling (*e.g.* goat, beaver), a familiar pet (*e.g.* dog), but every grocery store in Finland carries reindeer meat. It is a staple product, and if you like beef, you will almost certainly like reindeer when it is prepared well. Just try not to think about Santa's missing reindeer.

Smoked Kohlrabi Purée

Kohlrabi, 1 large or two small - peel with a knife

Milk (roughly 360mL or 12 oz)

Butter (roughly 30g or 1 oz)

Wood chips for smoking, ideally including a little juniper wood, or at least some juniper berries

ADDITIONAL NOTES

This is another example of what would be a minor plating element of a Michelin star caliber of dish. The only difference is that this would be processed using a machine called a Thermomix, which creates absolutely perfectly smooth glossy sauces - but the machine costs thousands of dollars and is rarely seen outside of the best restaurants.

Jamaican Jerk Chicken

2 t Allspice (whole berries, dried)

1-2" piece of Cinnamon (or 1 t powdered)

1 t Cloves

2 t Black Peppercorns

1 t Nutmeg

3/4 t Ginger, dried

1 1/2 T Brown Sugar

2 t Salt

6 Chicken Legs

30ml (1oz) Vegetable Oil

5-6 Green Onions (scallions)

1-2 Scotch Bonnet or Habeñero Peppers

5-6 Garlic cloves

60ml White Balsamic Vinegar (or malt vinegar)

Splash of malt liquor or beer

120g (4oz) Catsup

30ml (1oz) Soy Sauce

1T Dark Rum

Pistachio nuts and Cinnamon Sticks

ADDITIONAL NOTES

I received some criticism on this recipe for it not being hot enough to be authentic tasting, even though the flavor was otherwise well received. People - the answer is pretty simple. Just add more chilies if you want it even hotter! Personally, this is plenty hot for me, but if you grew up eating this sort of thing every day, this would seem mild, I suppose.

Mexican Style No-Fry Baked "Fried" Chicken

4 Chicken Quarters (legs and thighs)

30g (1 oz) Potato Chips (preferably onion flavor - NOT Pringles)

1 Green Chili Pepper, Jalapeño if you want it hotter

1 t Garlic Powder

3/4 t Cumin, ground

3/4 t Black Pepper, medium grind

3/4 t Thyme, dried

3/4 t Salt

Lime juice, fresh squeezed

A little fresh cilantro for garnish (optional)

ADDITIONAL NOTES

This video was mostly an experiment to see how people would react if I put a Rachael Ray type of 30 minute recipe up. It is much simpler than my other recipes, and it tastes good - but it isn't in the same league, I know. Everyone who actually tried it, liked it - but very few people bothered to make it, because this isn't the sort of fare that my channel is known for. Never the less, if you are short on time, or want to get your children involved in some cooking, here's a very simple and delicious recipe. I doubt that I will be posting anything else along these lines again. ☺

Kharcho (Georgian Lamb Soup)

800g (1 3/4lb) Lamb Leg (shank)

300g (10 oz) Tomato Purée (pasata)

120g (4 oz) Pomegranate Molasses

1 Onion, medium

2 t Khmeli-Suneli (Georgian spice mixture)

8 Garlic Cloves

1 t Smoked Paprika

1 T Coarse Salt

1-2 Red Chilies, dried

1" piece of Cinnamon stick

1/2 t Black Peppercorns

1/2 t Cumin Seeds

60g (2oz) Rice (I prefer Basmati, but it is not traditional)

1 bunch Cilantro, fresh (about 25g, or 3/4 oz)

Sunflower Oil (preferably unfiltered)

Peanut Oil, if possible

Red Wine Vinegar (just a tiny bit)

ADDITIONAL NOTES

This soup benefits from a long very slow simmer. I've let it sit at the back of the stove for up to 6 hours only barely bubbling, and the flavor only got better. Just don't boil it, or try to rush it.

Italian Pasta Bolognese

450g (1 lb) Beef Shortribs

400g (14 oz) Italian Tomato Purée (pasata)

300 ml (10 oz) Chicken Stock

1 head of Fennel

30g (1 oz) Shallots

Onions, Carrots, Celery Root, Garlic

60g (2 oz) Pancetta

Parmesan cheese (freshly grated)

Red Wine, dry

Paprika, Bay Leaves

Fresh herbs (basil, parsley, thyme) - optional

Black Pepper, Coarse Salt, Sugar

Olive Oil, Butter, Cream (or milk)

Tagliatelle or Pappardelle Pasta

ADDITIONAL NOTES

This recipe is reasonably straightforward, but perhaps what it best illustrates is how making advance preparations can produce a complex dish that tastes freshly made quickly on demand, which is how good restaurants operate. It is also something that virtually no cookbook or cooking show explains, but it is a useful skill for the home cook, too. Not only in case guests arrive unexpectedly, but also if you live alone and want a great meal in a hurry after a day at work. By doing the work ahead of time, you can turn out a dish that would take an hour or two to make from scratch, in 10 minutes.

Veal or Faux Veal Filling for Italian Pasta

360g (12oz) Ground Veal
-OR-
240g (8oz) Ground Beef, lean
120g (4oz) Ground Chicken, breast only
- OR SOME COMBINATION OF THE TWO TO MAKE 360g (12oz)

60g (2oz) Shallots
3-4 cloves of Garlic
1 1/2 t Mixed Peppercorns (or just white peppercorns)
2T Soy Sauce
2T Pantelleria Wine, or substitute Vin Santo, or Sauternes
3T Chives, chopped fine
30g Breadcrumbs
15g Parmesan Cheese, freshly grated

ADDITIONAL NOTES

The combination of soy sauce, chives and veal is one of my own inventions. In the right propotions, the flavor combination is stunning. It doesn't work quite as well wiith the combination of beef and chicken given here as an alternative, but veal is often unavailaablee for months at a time in Russia, and the name of this channel is "Cooking in Russia", and so I explain the measures that have to be taken, for better or worse.

Holiday "Campfire" Brussels Sprouts

Brussels Sprouts

Smoked Bacon or fine quality Italian Sopressata

Pistachio Nuts, shelled and chopped coarsely

Onion

Honey

Sherry Vinegar

Liquid Smoke (Mesquite)

Vegetable Oil

Tabasco Sauce (or a pinch of cayenne)

Soy Sauce

Liquid Smoke

MSG (or Accent Seasoning)

Pistachio Nut Oil (optional)

ADDITIONAL NOTES

This is a great side dish with roast meats, but it is at its finest when part of an elaborate plating, as one would arrange in a Michelin starred restaurant. That level of cooking is something that I intentionally avoid on my channel, because it is lengthy and intimidating, but if you are a serious chef, use some imagination and you can see how this would be a fantastic flavor component.

Italian Stuffed Shells

Veal (or Faux Veal) Filling - shown in another video
Italian Tomato Sauce - also shown in another video

Italian Pasta Shells (Conchiglioni Gigante)
Ricotta (fresh)
Mozzarella (fresh)
Egg Yolks
Chicken Stock
Olive Oil
Basil, fresh

ADDITIONAL NOTES

I reallty only provided this as a method of showcasing the *Veal (or Faux Veal) Filling* recipe with the soy sauce and chives (see index). It is a simple basic recipe, but tested and sure to produce good results.

Green Peppercorn Béarnaise Sauce

22g (3/4 oz) Shallots, minced

1/2-3/4 t Green Peppercorns, dried

60ml (2 oz) White Wine, a good oaky Chardonnay

30ml (1 oz) Red Wine Vinegar

1 t Tarragon (dried)

60-120g (2-4oz) Butter, depending on how thick you want it

2 Egg Yolks

ADDITIONAL NOTES

The quality of dried tarragon varies widely from brand to brand. The best are generally from France, with Sweden also making an outstanding product. Choosing a quality product here is essential.

Potato Gratin "Cake"

Red Potatoes, such as Klondike Rose
1 Onion, core removed (120g, or about 4 oz)
60g (2oz) Butter
60ml (2oz) White Wine, dry
30ml (1oz) Olive Oil
Rosemary, fresh
Garlic, 2 cloves
1/2 t White Pepper, ground

ADDITIONAL NOTES

This is another example of a dish that needs to be made a day
ahead of time (or more). It should be refrigerated overnight before
cutting it, and then slices reheated in a steam injection/convection
oven ideally (which is what commercial kitchens use), or failing that,
in your home oven on a very hot setting.

Golden Cauliflower Florets

1kg (2.2lb) Cauliflower, regular or (preferably) orange

30g (1oz) Butter

180g (6 1/2 oz) Onion, sliced

150ml (5 1/4 oz) Milk

150ml (5 1/4 oz) Chicken Stock

60g (2 oz) Kozstromskoy Cheese (substitute Jack)

1 t Sherry Vinegar

1/2 t Cumin, ground

1/2 t White Pepper, ground

1/2 t Thyme, dried (or 1 t fresh)

1/4 t Baking Soda

Flour

ADDITIONAL NOTES

This recipe is difficult to execute properly, so be warned. Most of the recipes I put up should be possible to get right the first time you make them if you pay attention. This is an exception to that. You will probably have to make this several times before you get it right.

I may take this video down in the near future and remake it to show how this can work best for a home kitchen. The method shown really only works in a commercial restaurant with an enormous deep fryer that can't be overloaded with water very easily.

Farfalle with Marinated Tomatoes from Calabria

4 Tomatoes, ripe and medium-size - best quality obtainable

90ml (3 1/4 oz) Red Wine Vinegar

1 t Marjoram, dried - or a couple of sprigs of fresh

1-2 Red Chilies (see text at start of this video)

2-3 Bay Leaves, dried

6-8 Cloves, whole (the spice, that is)

1 Garlic clove

2 Strips of Orange or Lemon Peel (see video)

1 1/2 T Salt

80g (2 3/4 oz) Farfalle (for 2 servings)

60g (2 oz) Onion, finely chopped

30g Parmesan, freshly grated

1 t Marjoram, dried

3-6 Garlic cloves, whole

3 T Olive Oil, extra virgin

1-2 t Parsley, chopped or torn

Sprigs of fresh Marjoram or Thyme for garnish (optional)

ADDITIONAL NOTES

This is a nice dish to make if you have your own tomato garden, because you can pickle the tomatoes and enjoy them after the season is over.

This is a great dish to make your own farfalle pasta for, too. It is an activity that you can teach children to do. Since most children won't enjoy the level of spicy heat in this dish, you can give them some that are cooked simply with butter and cheese.

Traditional Italian Ravioli from Scratch

Filling, such as Veal (or Faux Veal) Filling - shown in another video

INGREDIENTS FOR TRADITIONAL RAVIOLI
210g (7 1/2 oz) Flour (preferably 00, but AP is okay)
2 whole Eggs plus another Egg Yolk (extra large eggs)
1 T Olive Oil

INGREDIENTS FOR THINNER RAVIOLI
210g (7 1/2 oz) Flour, all purpose
2 Egg Yolks (extra large eggs)
70ml (2 1/2 oz) Water, ice cold
1 t Olive Oil

ADDITIONAL NOTES
Use dusting flour freely when rolling the dough, and keep long
strips covered with either cling film, or a very slightly damp towel
while you are working with the rest of the pasta. Practice makes
perfect - and that's really the bottom line here. What seems like a
difficult and laborios task the first couple of times you do it,
becomes like your morning commute to work after a while - you just
do it without even thinking about it.

Cheddar Ale Soup

120g (4 1/4 oz) Carrot

60g (2oz) Leek or Onion

4 Garlic cloves

90g (3 1/4 oz) Butter

4 T Flour

2 t Corn Starch

200ml (7 oz) Chicken Stock

300ml (10 1/2 oz) Milk

100g (3 1/2 oz) Cheddar, grated

250ml (8 3/4 oz) Ale of your choice (see note below)

1/2 t each White Pepper and Dry Mustard

ADDITIONAL NOTES

Be sure to watch my *12 Shades of Roux* video before attempting to make this soup, unless you are already an expert at roux.

Also, your choice of ale here is important. I've received email from people who were disappointed because they tried making this with things like Budweiser and Guinness. The best results will be with a quality ale that is not too strong in flavor, and not bitter.

Indian Red Curry Masala Paste

4 T Coconut, dried and unsweetened

2 T Sesame Seeds

4 T Coriander Seeds

2 T Cumin Seeds

1/2 t Cloves, whole (the spice - NOT garlic)

1/4 t Mustard Seeds

1/4 t Fenugreek, whole

1/4 t Black Peppercorns, whole

2 T Peanut Oil, or Vegetable Oil

90g (3 1/4 oz) Clarified Butter, or Ghee

250g (8 3/4 oz) Onion, coarsely diced

2 Bay Leaves

45g (1 1/2 oz) Garlic, chopped small

45g (1 1/2 oz) Ginger, chopped small

500g (17 1/2 oz) Tomato Purée, boxed

1 t Paprika

2 t Sugarasdfa

2 t Salt

ADDITIONAL NOTES

This is one of my most treasured recipes, partly stolen and partly invented over many years, including time I spent working in two different Indian restaurants. The results you will obtain are every bit as good as the finest Indian restaurant (better than the places that I worked, in fact). It is a laborious task to make, but the good thing is that once you have a jar of this in your refrigerator, it will keep for a couple of weeks (or more) and you can produce a wide variety of high quality Indian dishes easily (as shown in my other videos).

4 Curries from 1 Masala:
Spicy Red Lentil Dahl

45g (1 1/2 oz) Indian Red Curry Masala Paste - see separate video

100g (about 1/2 cup) Red Lentils

300ml (10 1/2 oz) Water

2 Green Chili Peppers (Serrano)

22g (3/4 oz) Butter or Ghee

30g (1 oz) Onion

Sprigs of Fresh Cilantro to garnish

ADDITIONAL NOTES

If you do not have the Red Curry Masala Paste from my other video, and you are in a pinch, you can cook down tomatoes with ginger, garlic and my Garam Masala spice blend (see index) to use as the base for this. It will not be the same sort of stellar dish, but it willl work if it is only going to be a side dish of a larger meal.

4 Curries from 1 Masala:
Coconut Curry Chicken

60g (2 oz) indian Red Curry Masala Paste - see separate video

2 Garlic Cloves

22g (3/4 oz) Peanut Oil (or substitute vegetable oil)

200g (7 oz) Chicken Thighs, boneless and skinless

75g (2 3/4 oz) Onion

30g (1 oz) Butter

120g (4 1/4 oz) Coconut Milk, canned unsweetened

1/2 t Curry Powder, Hot Madras (optional)

1-2 T Cilantro, fresh

Lemon Juice, fresh

COCONUT MILK

Although restaurants almost always use canned coconut milk, this dish especially benefits from making your own coconut milk from freshly grated coconut. You can also used packaged dessicated coconut, but then you result will be about like the canned product, so what's the point? Here's how to do it:

250g (8.8 oz)   Coconut, freshly grated

500ml (2 cups)   Boiling Water

Pour the water over the coconut and allow it to stand for 5 minutes. Now put it in a blender and purée for a full minute. Line a sieve with two layers of cheese cloth and pour the mixture into it. Pulling the ends of the cloth together at the top, gently squeeze the liquid through the cloth and the sieve. This will take several minutes. When you have most of the liquid squeezed out, discard the solids and store the coconut milk in a refrigerator for up to 5 days. If it tastes acidic, it's spoiled. You can store it in the freezer for months.

4 Curries from 1 Masala:
Bombay Potatoes

60g (2 oz) Indian Red Curry Masala Paste - see separate video

250g (8 3/4 oz) Potatoes, firm not starchy

30g (1 oz) Onion

2 Garlic Cloves

22g (3/4 oz) Peanut Oil (or substitute vegetable oil)

1/2 t Rosemary, dried

1 1/2 t Apricot Jam

1 t Cider Vinegar

3/4 t Coarse Salt (*not shown in the video)

Red Pepper Flakes (optional for more heat)

ADDITIONAL NOTES

Don't tell anyone what is in this, and they will enjoy it much more. The bizarre ingredients (apricot jam and rosemary) are so unexpected in an Indian dish, that almost no one would ever guess that they are there. All they sense is something delicious and very exotic, which is what great food should ellicit as a response - a sense of mystery and delight!

4 Curries from 1 Masala:
Tamarind-Chili Prawns

36g (1.25 oz) Indian Red Curry Masala Paste - see separate video
90g (3 1/4 oz) Prawns, peeled and deveined
45g (1 1/2 oz) Onion
1 T Tamarind Paste
Lime or Lemon Juice
2 T Vegetable Oil

ADDITIONAL NOTES

This is one of my absolute favorite Indian dishes, but unfortunately I realize that very few of my viewers will make this because of the work involved in the masala, the cost of the prawns, and the fact that you will need a little practice to cook them perfectly so that they are not tough. Still, if you put the time and money into this dish, you will be rewarded with a fabulous taste sensation.

Confit Lamb Bordelaise

1kg (2 1/4 lbs) Lamb Leg or Shoulder

30g (1 oz) Garlic

1 T Rosemary, dried - or fresh

Duck Fat (see video)

Vegetable Oil

80g (2 3/4 oz) Flour

200g (7 oz) Tomato Purée (pasata - not paste)

200g (7 oz) Onion

100g (3 1/2 oz) Celery

100g (3 1/2 oz) Carrot

100g (3 1/2 oz) Mushrooms

3-4 Garlic cloves

Bouquet Garni (parsley, bay, rosemary, peppercorns)

90ml Veal Stock (not essential)

90ml (3 oz) Red Wine, dry

45ml (1 1/2 oz) Sherry

FOR THE FONDANT POTATOES

Potatoes, peeled and cut like you see in the video

Chicken Stock

Garlic cloves

Butter, Vegetable Oil, Coarse Salt

ADDITIONAL NOTES

Use Demi-glace (see index) in place of the Veal Stock for better results. That is not a general rule of thumb, by the way - but it works here. What would be even better is Lamb Demi-glace. That's another video that will be made in the near future.

Lamb Bhuna

1.7kg (3 3/4 lbs) Lamb Leg or Shoulder

3 T Duck Fat, or Clarified Butter, or Ghee (see video)

10-12 cloves Garlic (used at different times)

500g (17 1/2 oz) Tomato Purée (pasata)

250g (9 oz) Onion

30g (1 oz) Ginger, fresh

2 T Yogurt, plain

30g (1 oz) Pecans (optional)

ROGAN JOSH SPICE BLEND

2 T Paprika

2 T Cumin Seeds

1 T + 1 t Coriander Seeds

6 Green Cardamom pods, whole

3 Brown Cardamom pods, whole

1 t Cinnamon, ground

1 t Ginger, dried (powder)

3/4 t Cloves, whole (the spice - not garlic)

1/2 t Turmeric, ground

2-3 Dried Red Chilies, stems removed

1 T Salt

ADDITIONAL NOTES

Use Kashmiri chilies for the "dried red chilies", and consider substituting your own dried sweet red chilies for the paprika in this recipe (as described in the front of this book - see index).

1 Rabbit as a 4 Course Meal for 2:
Advance Preparations

RABBIT STOCK REDUCTION
Back and trimmings from 1-1.5kg (2 1/2 lb) Rabbit
1 Onion
1 Carrot
1 Celery stalk
1 clove Garlic
10 Cloves, whole (the spice - not garlic)
1/2 t Mustard Seeds
1/2 t White Peppercorns
1/2 t Anise Seeds

FLAKY PASTRY DOUGH
180g (6 1/3 oz) Flour
100g (3 1/2 oz) Butter (first 50g then another 50g)
20g (3/4 oz) Bacon Drippings
Lemon, small slice

JUNIPER CREAM SAUCE

30g (1 oz) Shallot

30g (1 oz) Carrot

10 Juniper Berries

1/2 t White Peppercorns

1 Bay Leaf

120ml (4 oz) White Wine, dry

120ml (4 oz) Cream, 22% fat

1 T Rabbit Stock Reduction (the recipe is in this video)

1 t Gin

RABBIT MOUSSE

Rabbit Meat

1 Egg White

1 T Cream, 22% fat

1 T Breadcrumbs

pinch White Pepper, ground

pinch Nutmeg, freshly grated

1 Rabbit as a 4 Course Meal for 2:
Rabbit Tortellini in a Rabbit Reduction

Rabbit Mousse (recipe is in this video)

Pasta Dough, rolled as thin as possible (see below)

Garlic cloves

Sage, fresh

Olive Oil

PASTA DOUGH

The recipe calls for pasta dough. The standard rule of thumb is to use 1 egg per 100 grams (3.5 oz) of flour, plus a tiny bit of cold water to bring it together. For more detailed information watch my video, *Italian Ravioli from Scratch* (see index).

ADDITIONAL NOTES

Use the sage judiciously. Too much will overpower the rabbit. A good safe alternative is to deep fry the sage, and add the crisp bits to the tortellini on plating.

A "confetti" of brunois carrots (orange, yellow and purple) sprinkled around the edge of the plate makes a beautiful touch, but yellow and purple carrots are not available in Russia, so I couldn't show you that in the video.

1 Rabbit as a 4 Course Meal for 2:
Tart of Rabbit Braised in Red Wine

Rabbit, forelegs

Olive Oil

90ml (3 oz) Red Wine, dry

30g (1 oz) Shallot, diced

20g (3/4 oz) Carrot, diced

20g (3/4 oz) Mushroom, diced

30g (1 oz) Celery in large pieces

1 clove Garlic

Thyme, fresh

Flaky Pastry Dough (recipe is in this video)

Rabbit Stock Reduction (recipe is in this video)

1 Egg Yolk

1 T Chives, fresh

1 t Cognac

ADDITIONAL NOTES

I suggest a good Beaujolais for the wine. You don't want a wine that is too powerful, or it will bury the delicate flavor of the rabbit. Neither do you want anything too sweet, or it will be sickening. Beaujolais is the perfect balance.

The most important aspect of this tart is to be sure you remove all of the bones. Missing bone fragments is a mistake that even experienced cooks can make (and be promptly fired for), so don't underestimate the amount of patience and care it will take you to clean it up completely.

1 Rabbit as a 4 Course Meal for 2:
Saddle of Rabbit with Black Truffles

Saddle of Rabbit

Rabbit Mousse (recipe is in this video)

Flour

1 Egg, beaten

10g (1/3 oz) Dried Mushrooms (preferably Porcini)

1/2 t Coarse Salt

1/4 t Fennel Seeds

1 1/2 t Breadcrumbs

Black Truffle (or at least the oil)

ADDITIONAL NOTES

A word of caution when purchasing black truffles. The Chinese discovered a tuber that looks like a black truffle, but it has virtually no flavor. Because of corruption and poorly enforced trade laws, a tremendous volume of these flavorless truffles enter the market each year - often bearing labels that make them appear to be from Italy or France unless you read all of the fine print (which may be in Chinese, by the way). Know your source. Make sure that you are getting the real thing. If they have no flavor or aroma, you have been cheated, and sadly, that's very often the case.

1 Rabbit as a 4 Course Meal for 2:
Rabbit Haunch in Juniper Cream

Rabbit Haunch (rear leg and thigh)
Juniper Cream Sauce (recipe is in this video)
Duck Fat
Garlic Clove
Sage, fresh

Vegetables used for plating;
Asparagus, previously steamed partially
Carrot, cubed and previously steamed
Zucchini, cubed
Chives, fresh

ADDITIONAL NOTES

Most of this four-part recipe is fairly immune to the quality of the rabbit (within reason), but this is where you will observe the biggest difference. A domestic rabbit should not be too skinny, and must not have any visible signs of abuse. Look for dark spots on the flesh, or bruises. These are indications that the animal was kept in substandard conditiions. The same rule applies to chicken, and I plan to make a video showing how to identify birds that were raised in inhumane ways - but (believe it, or not) chickens and rabbits that were raised inhumanely are very hard to find as examples to show in Russian stores. I know it isn't the impression that most people have of Russia, but many of the farms are still small operations and the overcrowding and other practices that take place in larger countries don't happen here that much. I drive past one of the larger chicken farms here fairly often, and it is a vast expanse of land with thousands of chickens roaming completely free.

Massaman Chicken Curry

Spice Blend (see video):

1 t. Green Cardamom Pods

1 t. Cumin Seeds

1 t. Coriander Seeds

2.5cm (1 inch) Cinnamon Stick

1 Star Anise

2 Bay Leaves

1 1/2 t. Turmeric, ground

1/2 t. Fenugreek, ground

100g (3 1/2 oz) Green Chilies (or less)

60g (2 oz) Carrot

1 bunch Cilantro, fresh

400g Chicken, boneless, skinless thighs

300g Potatoes, peeled

70g (2 1/2 oz) Shallots

30g (1 oz) Ginger

30g (1 oz) Garlic

30g (1 oz) Lemongrass, peeled

1 T Basil, dried (or 3T fresh Thai Basil)

2 T Dark Brown Sugar

1 T Nam Pla (Thai Fish Sauce)

45g (1 1/2 oz) Cashews, shelled

400ml (1 can) Coconut Milk, unsweetened

120ml (4 oz) Chicken Stock, ideally homemade

1 Lime

2 T Peanut Oil

Turkey Tetrazzini

700-800g (about 26oz) Turkey Breast

1/4 Onion

2-3 cloves Garlic

Bay Leaf

Olive Oil

Milk

140g (5 oz) Mushrooms

45g (1 1/2 oz) Almonds

30-45g (1 - 1 1/2 oz) Parmesan

30-45ml (1 - 1 1/2 oz) White Wine, dry

150g (5 oz) Spaghettini #3

Parsley

ADDITIONAL NOTES

I was surprised at the lack of response to this video, but I think the problem is that the recipe name has such a bad reputation now that there's now way to ressurect it among the general public. That's unfortunate, because it is delicious and relatively easy to prepare.

Chinese Duck with Pancakes
using Confit Duck

Confit Duck Legs

190g (7 oz) Mandarin Orange segments (fresh - not canned)

3 strips Orange Zest

80g (3 oz) Granny Smith Apple

40g (1 1/2 oz) Carrot

40g (1 1/2 oz) Onion

40g (1 1/2 oz) Ginger

1/2 t Coriander Seeds

1/2 t Sichuan Peppercorns, whole

1 T Rice Vinegar

60ml (2 oz) Soy Sauce

60g (2 oz) Dark Brown Sugar, ideally Cassonade

350ml (12 1/2 oz) Chicken or Duck Stock

2 Dried Red Chilies

1 Star Anise, whole

Hoisin Sauce

Sesame Oil

Scallions

PANCAKES

30g (1 oz) Rice Flour

30g (1 oz) All Purpose Flour

1 Egg

1 t Salt

150ml Milk

Vegetable Oil or Duck Fat

"Illegal Sexy Legs"
Spicy Chicken Drumsticks

8 Chicken Drumsticks (about 900g / 2lbs)

4-5 Garlic cloves

2 T Coarse Salt

1 T Paprika (Spanish Smoked, or regular, or a mix)

2 T Sugar

1 Habeñero Chili

2 Bay Leaves

Vegetable Oil

Scallions (for plating)

SPICY HOT GLAZE

100ml (3 1/2 oz) Red Wine Vinegar

100ml (3 1/2 oz) Chicken Stock

60g (2 oz) Red Onion

30g (1 oz) Sugar

Red Chili Peppers or Habeñeros - to taste

25g (just under 1 oz) Butter

ADDITIONAL NOTES

This recipe is at its best when you pump up the heat to the point of requiring vast amounts of beer to wash down. For Russians, that doesn't take much heat, because they aren't used to spicy food as a general rule. If you are used to spicy food, crank up the heat on this one.

Savory Mushroom and Olive Bread Pudding

350g (12 oz) Mushrooms

100g (3 1/2 oz) Shallots (or onion)

90ml (3 oz) Cream, 22% fat

30ml (1 oz) Chicken Stock (or Mushroom Stock)

100g (3 1/2 oz) Bread, stale

30-60g Green Olives, ideally from Calabria, Italy

2 Eggs, whole

2 T Butter

2 T Olive Oil

1 t MSG, or Accent (optional)

ADDITIONAL NOTES

The quality of the ingredients you use here will determine whether this is good or phenomenal. Although I showed this in the video using ordinary champignon mushrooms, this really shines with an assortment of wild mushrooms. In that case you may want to try black oil cured olives.

Composed Asparagus Salad

Asparagus, fresh
Chicken Stock
Potatoes, preferably Yukon Gold
Black Truffle Oil
Hardboiled Eggs
Basil, fresh leaves
Parmigiano-Reggiano Cheese

THE DRESSING
15g (1/2 oz) Shallots, peeled and chopped
8-10 Basil Leaves, fresh
45g (1 1/2 oz) White Balsamic Vinegar
45g (1 1/2 oz) Olive Oil, extra-virgin
45g (1 1/2 oz) Mayonnaise

ADDITIONAL NOTES

This salad actually won a rather impressive award for the American National Culianry Team. The only sigificant difference to this recipe is that I left out the black truffles (substituting black truffle oil) and specified a commercial mayonaisse instead of telling you to make your own.

A note on black truffle oil, too. While much of it is nothing more than a chemical additive in olive oil, you can absolutely get the real thing if you are willing to pay for it. Look for the high priced products imported from France and Italy.

Russian Fish Mousse with Caviar

200g (7 oz) Fennel

30g (1 oz) Shallots

30ml (1 oz) White Wine, dry

200g (7 oz) Cod - or half cod and half sea scallops (much better)

2 Egg Whites

2 T Dill and Parsley (mixture)

1 t Dijon Mustard

45g (1 1/2 oz) Cream

Zucchini (see video)

Chives, fresh

Olive Oil, Sugar, Salt, Pepper

GARNISH

Caviar

Chickpeas (Garbanzo), canned

45ml (1 1/2 oz) Milk

1 Egg Yolk

1 1/4 t. Turmeric

1 t Parsley, dried

1 T Rice Flour

1/2 t Salt

ADDITIONAL NOTES

The quality of the caviar on top of this makes all of the difference.
This dish is about the caviar, despite it being physically smaller than
the other elements on the plate.

Fettuccine Alfredo

Fresh Fettuccine
Butter
Parmigiano-Reggiano, freshly grated
A touch of cream (optional)

FETTUCCINE PASTA
1 Onion, medium
1 Celery stalk
5-6 cloves Garlic
2 sprigs Parsley, fresh
1/4 t Turmeric
300g (10.6 oz) Flour
2 Egg Yolks

ADDITIONAL NOTES
This dish is very different with dried pasta. It was created for fresh
pasta. The original version is very heavy, and so I strongly suggest
thinning it out with cream. I provided the original method for the
stake of historical accuracy.

Fresh Garden Vegetable Terrine

1 Zucchini, large (as described in the video)

2 Red Bell Peppers

2 Carrots, cut in 1.3mm slices lengthwise

1 Eggplant, cut in 3mm slices

250g (9 oz) Spinach, fresh

30g (1 oz) Shallots, minced

60ml (2 oz) White Wine, dry

Goat Cheese, sliced (or use dollops of Ricotta)

3 T Chicken Stock or Vegetable Stock, thick

Nutmeg, Salt, Pepper

Olive Oil

ADDITIONAL NOTES

Terrines can be beautiful and produce stunning plating elements for beautiful presentations. This one is really a beginner type

Coq au Vin

2 - 2 1/4 kg (4 1/2 - 5 lb) Chicken

2 t Mixed Peppercorns (black, white, green, pink)

Dried Herbs: Rosemary, Chervil, Bay Leaf

Fresh Thyme (used in two places - see video)

Flour

200g (7 oz) Bacon

500ml (17 1/2 oz) Red Wine, dry (see video)

200ml Chicken Stock, preferably homemade

220g (8 oz) Mushrooms, small or quartered

100g (3 1/2 oz) Shallots

30g (1 oz) Garlic cloves

1-2 T Cognac

ADDITIONAL NOTES

There are a great many ways to prepare this dish. The one I showed in this video is fairly simple and straightforward. I will be making a more advanced version of this recipe in the near future, because this is a classic that warrants more attention.

French Chicken Fricassee
in Loïc Raison Cider

4 Chicken Thighs, skin-on

1-2 Carrots (depending on size)

4 Shallots

160ml (5 1/2 oz) Loïc Raison Cider, Brut

30ml (1 oz) Cream

1 t Dijon Mustard, or other quality mustard

1 T Dark Brown Sugar

1 T Lemon Juice

120ml (4 1/4 oz) Chicken Stock, preferably homemade

Marjoram, fresh sprigs

Vegetable Oil

ADDITIONAL NOTES

In my opinion, this dish only really works with Loïc Raison Cider. If you can't get the real thing, make something else instead.

The term fricassee is one that is seldom heard these days, and even less frequently used correctly. It is a dish that is braised on top of the stove with a cream based sauce. Rabbit is the most traditional meat for this application. Why the stovetop and not the oven? Because you have to keep checking it until it is tender but not falling apart. Dragging it out of the oven again and again is impractical, and it doesn't need the ultra-even heat that the oven provides, the way that red meat does.

Shrimp Arrabbiata
with Angel Hair Pasta

370g (13oz) Cherry Tomatoes

60-70g (2oz) Bacon, smokey

1 whole head of Garlic

140g (5oz) Onion

90ml White Wine, ideally Italian Soave

1 t Cognac (optional)

Lemon, fresh

Thyme, fresh

Parmegiano-Reggianno Cheese

100-120g (4oz) Angel Hair Pasta

8-10 Large Shrimp, raw with the shell on (see note below)

ADDITIONAL NOTES

You will need to peel and devein the shrimp yourself because you will be using the shrimp shells for this recipe. In general I always suggest buying shrimp with the shells and tails on for several reasons. First, they are usually less expensive. Second, you get the shells and tails to make shrimp stock with. Third, they are better quality because they are handled less and the shells protected them during shipping and freezing.

Caprese Salad
with Modern Plating

Cherry Tomatoes, vine ripe

Mozzarella, fresh (wet packed)

Cream

Capers, ideally salt-packed

Garlic clove

Olive Oil, high quality extra-virgin

Basil, fresh

Salt and Pepper

ADDITIONAL NOTES

The success of this dish depends entirely on the quality of the ingredients. If you make this using ordinary supermarket tomatoes and poor quality olive oil, it will be mediocre at best. A simple dish like this has no place for inferior products to hide. It is a showcase for the finest products you can obtain.

Carne Guisado

1 kg (2.2 lbs) Beef Shortribs
300g (10.5 oz) Tomato Purée (pasata)
120g (4.25 oz) Onion, sliced
* 6 Dried Chilies (see note below)
1 Head of Garlic, peeled and trimmed
1 T Flour - preferably Corn Flour
1 t each Salt, Black Pepper, Cayenne
Bay Leaf
1/2 t Cinnamon, ground
1 T Cumin, ground
1 T Oregano, dried
45g (1.5 oz) Sweetened Condensed Milk

ADDITIONAL NOTES

Chilies that are good to combine include a mix of Ancho, Mulato, New Mexico and Ají Panca. You can substitute a fresh jalapeño for one of them, if you like. Don't use habeñeros or chipotles for this.

This is a good example of a dish that is so delicious that it just as popular with the poor as it is with the wealthy in Central America. The basic flavor combination is a timeless classic with the half twist of condensed milk and a whole bouquet of flavorful chili peppers.

Jewel Box Chicken Tagine

3/4 t Fenugreek

1 t Sichuan Peppercorns

1 t Coarse Salt

2-3 Red Chilies, dried

4cm (1 1/2 inches) Cinnamon Stick

1/2 t Nutmeg, ground

15g (1/2 oz) Dark Brown Sugar

1/2 t Garlic Powder

900 g (2 lb) Chicken Thighs, skin-on

60g (2 oz) Shallot, coarsely chopped

150g (5 oz) Dried Apricots

150ml (5 oz) Chicken Stock

120g (4 oz) Red Bell Pepper, diced

1/2 - 3/4 t Orange Zest

2 T Sugar, white

2 T Cider Vinegar

ADDITIONAL NOTES

This is not authentic anything, despite being dressed up as Morrocan. Leave out the red chili peppers, and you have a dish that is a nearly universal favorite with children.

One of the things I really like about this dish is that it shows how interesting Sichuan peppercorns and fenugreek are together as a team. It is not a pairing that you encounter very often, if ever anywhere else, for that matter. Note to self: this needs to be exploited more in the future, because this combination is both intriguing and delicious.

Boar Taco Tapas

800g (1.75 lb) Boar (or beef) Steak

200g Onion, coarsely chopped

200g Tomato Purée (pasata)

6 Garlic Cloves

2 Dried Chilies (mild)

1 1/2 t Smoked Paprika (Pimenton)

1 T Vegetable Oil

1/2 t Allspice

1/2 t Cloves

1/2 of a Star Anise

1 t Black Peppercorns

1 Dried Red Chili Pepper

1 t Coarse Salt

ADDITIONAL NOTES

These days a successful restaurant in Barcelona must be doing something right because the compeitition is fierce. There has been an ongoing struggle with the wild boar population in the surrounding area - so much so that wild boars have been seen roaming the streets of the city in recent times. The meat is usually stewed or braised.

This is best enjoyed as a small tapas plate with friends. It is rather heavy and rich to try and make a complete meal out of on its own.

Lamb Moussaka

500g (17 1/2 oz) ground Lamb, or enough to provide 500g meat

250ml (1 cup) Red Wine, dry

300g (10oz) Tomato Purée (pasata)

200g (8oz) Onion, sliced

8 cloves Garlic

325g (11 1/2 oz) Potatoes, sliced 3mm thick

1 Eggplant, peeled

45g (1 1/2 oz Butter)

2 T Flour

500ml (2 cups) Milk

160g (5 1/2 oz) Mozzarella, shredded

15g (1/2 oz) Parmesan Cheese, to be grated

2 t Sesame Seeds

1 t Fenugreek, whole

1 t Thyme, dried

1 t Sumac

1 Bay Leaf

1 t Coarse Salt

1 t Coarse Black Pepper

ADDITIONAL NOTES

This is another dish that has been tailored for restaurant use, in case I didn't make this clear in the video. The optimum result is obtained by making it a day or two ahead, then when you actually want to eat it, cutting a slice and blasting it in a steam convection oven (if you are in a restaurant with that sort of equipment) or roasting it a second time in your oven.

Salmon in Leek Confit Wrapper

100ml (3 1/2 oz) Red Wine, dry

60g (2 oz) Onion, coarsely chopped

1 clove Garlic, chopped

1/2 t Black Peppercorns, whole

1 Bay Leaf

100ml Fish Stock (or from concentrate)

30ml (1 oz) Soy Sauce

30ml (1 oz) Rice Wine Vinegar

30ml (1 oz) Red Wine, dry

30g (1 oz) Daikon Radish, coarsely chopped

30g (1 oz) Dark Brown Sugar

1 1/2 t Catsup

3 T Basil, fresh or (much better) Shiso Leaf

Leeks

Scallions or Micro Chives

ADDITIONAL NOTES

This recipe is difficult to execute properly, so be warned. Most of the recipes I put up should be possible to get right the first time you make them if you pay attention. This is an exception to that.

One of the problems in trying to show elegant Michelin star quality dishes in videos is that to show ALL of the items that end up on the final plate, the video would be hours long. This is one of the elements from such a plate.This is not intended to be served by itself, but rather as a single item on a plate with other interesting components that vary in taste and texture. I always include nigiri sushi with this, for example. This dish will disappoint if you try to make a meal of it by itself.

Salad of Sweet Potato Curry

30g (1 oz) Ghee or clarified butter

1 t Cumin Seeds, whole

70g (2 1/2 oz) Onion, sliced thinly

70g (2 1/2 oz) Red Bell Pepper

15g (1/2 oz) Garlic, cut finely

15g (1/2 oz) Ginger, cut finely

200g (7 oz) Sweet Potatoes

400g (14 oz) Tomatoes, skinned & diced (canned is ok)

1 t Tamarind paste

Cilantro, fresh

Mustard

Lemon Juice

ADDITIONAL NOTES

As in the case of the *Salmon in Leek Confit Wrapper*, this is really best suited to being a single element on a plate with other components. This one does stand up to being a dish on its own, but it is much better as a quenelle alongside of other plating elements.

My favorite brand of tamarind paste is Blue Dragon. There are some brands that are absolutely miserable, so beware. Preparing your own from the tamarind and hot water will not even come close to the taste you get from Blue Dragon's product - but I must add that it is the *only* product from Blue Dragon that I would recommend.

Stuffed Mushrooms
with Shrimp and Bacon

8 Large Mushrooms

1/2 Lemon (for juice)

45g (1 1/2 oz) Bacon

60g (2oz) Red Onion, diced

22g (3/4 oz) Garlic, chopped coarsely

60g (2 oz) Shrimp, shelled

1/2 t Paprika

30ml (1 oz) White Wine, dry

2 Egg Yolks

2 T Bread Crumbs

Cayenne to taste (from a pinch to 1/2 teaspoon)

Parmesan Cheese

ADDITIONAL NOTES

Multiply the ingredients to scale this up, otherwise it will seem like a lot of work for a small amount of food, and it won't take you much longer to make two or three times the amount.

Chicken Masala Flatbread Pizza

Whole Wheat Dough for Flatbread Pizza (see separate video)

350-400g (14 oz) Chicken, boneless, skinless

2 Green Serrano Chilies

70g (2 1/2 oz) Onion

15g (1/2 oz) Garlic cloves

15g (1/2 oz) Ginger, peeled and chopped

2 T Yogurt (full fat)

30ml (1 oz) Lemon Juice

30g (1 oz) Butter

70g (2 1/2 oz) Tomato Purée

30-40g (1 1/2 oz) Cilantro, fresh

1 t Mint, dried

Additional Cilantro for topping

Yogurt (full fat)

Kostromskoy cheese, or substitute Jack

GARAM MASALA SPICE

2 t Cumin Seeds

8cm (3") Cinnamon Stick, broken up

1 t Cloves, whole (the spice - not garlic)

6-8 Green Cardamom pods

3-4 Dried Red Chilies

1 Star Anise, whole

1/2 t Black Peppercorns

2 t Paprika

1 t Ginger, ground

1/2 t Nutmeg, ground

1 t Brown Sugar

Whole Wheat Dough
for Flatbread or Pizza

200ml (7 oz) Water

1 T fresh Yeast, or 1 packet dried

1 1/2 t Salt

1-2 T Olive Oil

300g (10 1/2 oz) Flour - see below

1 T white AP Flour

ADDITIONAL NOTES

Use fresh yeast, if at all possible.

A little known fact is that not all whole wheat flours are created equal. In fact, most contain other ingredients such as malt. Because "whole wheat" is not a term recognized by the FDA, it is not regulated. What is regulated is "wholemeal flour", which is what most consumers mistakingly think that they are getting when they pick out whole wheat. In general, the best source of wholemeal flour is Italy, because there it is tightly controlled, regulated and inspected. The "whole wheat" flour sold in the United States is often almost impossible to use for making quality pizza or flatbread.

Jambalaya

140g (5 oz) Rice - I like Carnarolli or Jasmine

140g (5 oz) Smoked Sausage, boiled first

140g (5 oz) Chicken Breast, raw - cubed

140g (5 oz) Large Shrimp, raw

70g (2 1/2 oz) Canadian Bacon, diced

70g (2 1/2 oz) Bay Shrimp

70g (2 1/2 oz) Red Bell Pepper, cubed

70g (2 1/2 oz) Onion, diced

30g (1 oz) Celery, diced

15g (1/2 oz) Garlic, cut in pieces

1 Jalapeño Chili (or Serrano) diced with seeds

2-3 Tomatoes, canned (whole)

350ml (1 1/2 C) Chicken Stock

30ml (1 oz) White Wine, dry

Smoked Paprika, Garlic Powder, Red Pepper Flakes

ADDITIONAL NOTES

Andouille sausage is the obvious choice if you can get it, unfortunately it is nonexistent in Russia (and pretty much the rest of the world, with the only exception I know of being Barcelona). The next best thing is making your own sausage, but this is a process that few people are going to undertake, I realize. Kielbasa is an acceptable and readily available ingredient you can use.

In case you are wondering, the purpose of the bay shrimp are to elevate the shrimp taste in the dish at an affordable price with no work.

Pain Perdu as a Dessert

30g (1 oz) Butter, melted

1 Egg, whole

60ml (2 oz) Milk

1 T Orange Zest

1 T Sugar

1 T Corn Starch

1/8 t Nutmeg, ground

Bread - unsliced (see video)

Additional melted butter

TOPPING

350-400g Heavy Cream

120g (4 oz) Cream Cheese, softened

60g (2 oz) Sugar

3/4 t Vanilla Extract

Fresh Strawberries

Grand Marnier Liqueur (optional)

ADDITIONAL NOTES

Vanilla extract is virtually unheard of in Russia. The only thing sold
in is the chemical, 4-Hydroxy-3-methoxybenzaldehyde, better
known as vanillin in food manufacturing. You can find vanilla beans
with a little searching, but they are invariably old and dried out. So I
started making my own by cutting up some of the dried beans and
leaving them in a jar with vodka. As months went by, I added more
beans and more vodka, eventually ending up with a solution that's
better tasting than the commercial vanilla extract you can buy. At
this point I have dozens of beans that are just barely covered with a
layer of vodka, so you can imagine the intensity of the flavor.

Russian Pierogi Dough

200ml (7 oz) Milk

3 t Sugar

2 T Yeast, live - or 1 packet dried active

310 - 350g (11 - 12 oz) Flour SEE NEXT PAGE

1 Egg, whole - extra large

1 t Baking Powder, double acting

3/4 t Salt

* 1/4-1/2 t MSG (Monosodium Glutemate) - optional

Additional egg yolk for glazing - see video

ADDITIONAL NOTES

Use fresh yeast, if at all possible.

You can also deep fry these for a delicious (though completely non-authentic) type of bun. There are no traditional deep fried Russian foods, because oil was a very expensive commodity until recently.

Baked Mushroom Pierogi

Pierogi Dough (see separate video)

350g (12.5 oz) Mushrooms

60g (2 oz) Onion, grated

4 cloves Garlic

30g (1 oz) Vegetable Oil

1 T fat or 2 T Butter

1 t Dill, dried (or 1 1/2 T fresh dill, minced)

* 1/2 - 1 T Salsa Bravas (optional - see separate video)

ADDITIONAL NOTES

Wild mushrooms are almost the only kind ever used to make this. In fact, most Russians do not buy champignons (button mushrooms) at all. They forage mushrooms when they are in season and either freeze them, or preserve them with pickling or salting to use through the rest of the year. Store-bought mushrooms are seen as both a waste of money (since they are free in the woods once each year) and having no flavor (which is true by comparison). However, having said that, this filling is still good even if you don't have porcini mushrooms to make it with.

Salsa Bravas

60g (2 oz) Red Onion

2 Red Serrano Chilies, whole (22g or 3/4oz)

30ml (1oz) Vegetable Oil

2 t Smoked Paprika (Spanish Pimenton)

1 t Cumin Seeds, whole

300-350g (11 1/2 oz) Tomatoes, ripe

30g (1 oz) Celery

22-30g (3/4 to 1 oz) Garlic cloves

1 t Salt

1/2 t Black Peppercorns, whole

1 t Sugar

ADDITIONAL NOTES

This sauce can be streaked on a plate beneath meat, vegetables or seafood as part of an elaborate plating, or used as a kind of Spanish ketchup on fried potatoes, as tapas bars serve. Finally, this is a useful item to keep on hand in the refrigerator as a component for other sauces. A dab of this will liven up many savory dishes.

Banana Chutney

120g (4 1/4 oz) Banana, ripe

45g (1 1/2 oz) Vegetable Oil

1 t Mustard Seeds, whole

60g (2 oz) Onion

30g (1 oz) Ginger, peeled

1 Red Serrano Chili

1 Cinnamon Stick

1 t Turmeric, ground

1 t Salt

120ml (4 1/4 oz) Cider Vinegar

2 T Sugar

ADDITIONAL NOTES

Forget what you think you know about bananas. This versatile fruit is used in many applications outside of Europe and North America.

Like the *Salsa Bravas* recipe (see index), this is useful both as a condiment directly as well as a means of adjusting the flavor profile of other sauces. A small amount of this added to a sauce will provide complexity in the same way that Angostura bitters are used in cocktails.

Try mixing this with peanut butter and yogurt for a party dip, too.

Hawaiian Style Salmon Ceviche

300g (10-11 oz) Salmon

30g (1 oz) Banana Chutney (see separate video)

30g (1 oz) Lime Juice

2 T Red Onion, sliced 0.5mm on a mandoline

Scallions, chopped fine

Cilantro, chopped fine

2 T Coconut, dried and unsweetened

ADDITIONAL NOTES

The success of this dish depends on the freshness of the fish and the amount of time it spends in the marinade. You can use other types of fish, but if the fish is too mild, you won't taste anything other than the banana chutney. If the fish is too strong tasting, such as mackeral, it will clash with the banana. Salmon is a good choice because it is just assertive enough to be tasted.

Shrimp Flambéed in Dark Rum

Shrimp, large raw
Rum, dark (preferably Cuban)
Angostura Bitters
Tabasco (optional)
Cilantro for garnish (optional)
Red Pepper Flakes (optional)

SAUCE

90g (3 oz) Shallots, or red and brown onions
30g (1 oz) Butter, clarified
1 Cardamom pod, brown
1 Bay Leaf
2-3 Garlic cloves
1 t Ginger, grated
1 T Coconut, dried and unsweetened
200g (7 oz) Cooked Apricots (see separate video)
1/2 t Fenugreek, ground
120ml (4 oz) Chicken Stock, dark
1/2 t Cayenne

ADDITIONAL NOTES

This is *not* a foolproof dish, as most of my other recipes are (or at least I try to make them foolproof by providing detailed directions). This will require some skill in the final stage to get the shrimp cooked perfectly and produce a clean result, but this is an outstanding and theatrical dish, especially if you enjoy tropical cocktails.

Perfect Roast Chicken

Chicken between 2.2 and 2.5kg (5 to 5 1/2 lbs)

1 t Mixed Peppercorns (black, white, green, pink)

1 t Tarragon, dried

1 t Thyme, dried

1 t Garlic powder

1 t Dark Brown Sugar, ideally Muscovado

1/2 t Chervil, dried

1/2 t Paprika

2 t Salt

1 Bay Leaf

1/2 Knorr brand Chicken Stock cube (see video)

25 ml (3/4 oz) Lemon Juice

25 ml (3/4 oz) Olive Oil

ADDITIONAL NOTES

Ideally you want to use a roasting pan for this to keep the chicken up away from the bottom of the pan, otherwise the skin will not be crispy on all sides.

You can certainly change the compositioin of the herbs to suit your own tastes. This mixture resulted from a tasting that I did at a restaurant for 25 guests who were each given six differently seasoned chicken pieces to vote on. A total of 16 of them voted this one as their favorite, but 2 voted it as their least favorite. One of those individuals said their most favorite was this same mixture but with cayenne replacing the tarragon. The other person said their favorite was

Stovetop Baked Stuffing

160g (5 1/2 oz) Bread (with any thick crusts trimmed off)

60ml Olive Oil, extra virgin

60g (2 oz) Red Bell Pepper

30g (1 oz) Garlic cloves

3/4 t Rosemary, dried

3/4 t. Paprika

1/2 t Salt

200g (7 oz) Celery

180g (6 1/2 oz) Mushrooms

160g (5 1/2 oz) Onions

45g (1 1/2 oz) Butter

2 T Sage, fresh

* Other fresh herbs may also be added

120ml (4 oz) Chicken Stock, dark

2 Eggs (1 whole and 1 yolk-only)

White Pepper, preferably freshly ground

30ml (1 oz) Vermouth, dry (optional)

ADDITIONAL NOTES

The type of bread you use here will make a huge difference in the results you obtain. You want a bread with body and character. If you try to make this with sandwich loaf bread, it will be mushy and terrible. I suggest using my *Magic No-Kneading Bread* recipe (see index).

Tonkatsu Pork and Sauce

Pork Chops, thin and boneless
Flour
Corn Starch
Egg
Panko Bread Crumbs
Vegetable Oil for frying

SAUCE
120g (4 1/4 oz) Golden Apple
90g (3 oz) Mushrooms
90g (3 oz) Tomatoes
1 Garlic clove
1 T (15ml) Rice Wine Vinegar
1 t Dark Brown Sugar, ideally Cassonade
90ml (3 oz) Water
1 T (15ml) Worcestershire Sauce

ADDITIONAL NOTES
You may substitute pear for apple. This is a common variation.
Use a Jaccard device on the pork.

Aztek Plov

350g (12.3 oz) Cooked Basmati Rice (see separate video)

45g (1.5 oz) Butter

10g (2 T) Cumin, ground

1 Jalapeño Pepper

60g (2 oz) Onion

22g (3/4 oz) Garlic cloves

45ml (1.5 oz) Lime Juice, fresh

180-200g (6.7 oz) Chicken Breast

100g (3.5 oz) Mayonnaise

45g (1.5 oz) Monterrey Jack Cheese, grated

1/2 t Oregano, dried

Salt, Pepper, Vegetable Oil

Cilantro

Lime Wedges

Green Tabasco Sauce

ADDITIONAL NOTES

In the restaurant where I developed this item, we would include the drippings from the chicken, as well as chopping up the skin to mix in with the rice. It isn't healthy, of course, but it is even more delicious that way. This is the sort of thing that restaurants do. Not only to minimize waste, but the priority being on flavor, because that's what brings customers back.

I actually use a bit less lime juice for Russians, because they are very sensitive to anything acidic. Almost anything that tastes sour, is perceived as spoiled, so you have to be very careful with citrus and vinegar or the reaction will be to spit it out, believing that it's rancid.

Tefteli
Russian Chicken and Pork Meatballs

350-400g (12-14oz) Pork trimmings

350-400g (12-14oz) Chicken breast meat

300g (11 oz) Onions (in all)

60g (2oz) Bread Crumbs (see video)

30ml (1oz) Lemon Juice, fresh

1/2 t Baking Soda (not baking powder)

30ml (1 oz) Sherry Vinegar

3/4 t Dill, dried (or 2 T fresh)

Sugar, Salt, Pepper

ADDITIONAL NOTES

The recipe that I provided here contains twice the amount of lemon juice that I would use for Russians, who are very sensitive to sour tastes. I also explained on the previous page concerning the *Aztek Plov* recipe. Most of the world is used to citrus and/or vinegar in food, but those flavors never really made it to Russia, where bland, spice-free, neutral-tasting food has dominated for centuries.

Rulka

Rulka (ham hock - see video), preferably at least 2kg (4.5 lbs)
Onion, large
2 T Smoked Paprika (Pimentón)
1 t whole Cloves (the spice)
1 t Black Peppercorns, whole
1 whole head Garlic
1 bottle Beer (your choice of what type)
Bay Leaves

SAUCE
110g (4 oz) Red Onion
60g (2 oz) Red Bell Pepper
22g (3/4 oz) Garlic, peeled
180g (6 1/2 oz) Tomato puréed (pasata)
1 t Cloves, whole (the spice)
1 T Adjika (Georgian spice paste)
90ml (3 oz) Beer (or substitute water)
60g (2 oz) Sugar
30ml (1 oz) Lemon Juice

ADDITIONAL NOTES
Precooked Rulka is sold in many grocery stores in Russia, especially in summer, but it is nothing like this! Chewy and not well seasoned. Adjika is a common ingredient in eastern Europe and available online, as well as Russian specialty stores in larger cities.

Cream of Celery Soup
with Lobster or Crab

300g (10 1/2 oz) Celery

115g (4 oz) Onion

300ml (10 1/2 oz) Chicken Stock (see note below)

90ml (3 oz) White Wine, dry

2-3 Garlic cloves

1/2 t Mustard Seeds (preferably brown)

1 Bay Leaf

Vegetable Oil

1 t. Sugar

100ml (3 1/2 oz) Cream

* Cooked Lobster or Crab claw meat (optional)

Chives, fresh (as garnish)

ADDITIONAL NOTES

This is a delcous soup without the seafood addition. But if you are going to use lobster or crab, you should subsittute a shellfish stock for the chicken stock in the recipe. A divine version of this is made with lobster stock and lobster claw meat. A tiny bit of paprika dusted around the edge of the bowl adds a nice complimentary aroma.

Fried Polenta
with Mushrooms

105g (3 3/4 oz) Polenta
45g (1 1/2 oz) Butter
2 T Flour
150ml (5 oz) Milk
200ml (7 oz) Water or dilute chicken stock
3/4 t Salt
Olive Oil (for frying)
Mozzarella (optional)
Parmesan Cheese, fresh

Chanterelle Mushrooms
Garlic
Rosemary (optional)
Black Truffle Oil (optional)

ADDITIONAL NOTES

Although most people are not aware of it, Parmigiano Reggiano comes in different ages. If it is aged less than 18 months, it is marked "export", which is what most packaged products are. Next up is "extra" which must be aged for 18 months. Beyond 24 months and it is "stravecchio", which I have seen all the way up to 6 years. As the cheese ages, it becomes more complex and deeper. This dish benefits greatly from the most aged parmesan you can obtain.

Coquilles St. Jacques
(Two Ways)

200g (7oz) Scallops (weight after drying)

150g (5 1/4 oz) Mushrooms (see notes below)

60g (2 oz) Scallions (green onions)

200ml (7 oz) White Wine, dry

150ml (5 1/4 oz) Cream, or Half & Half

30ml (1 oz) Lemon Juice, fresh

1 Garlic clove

1 Bay Leaf

1/2 t. Paprika (only for fusion version)

1/2 t. White Pepper, fresh ground

30ml (1 oz) Cognac

45ml (1 1/2 oz) Sherry, dry

15ml (1/2 oz) Sherry or Sauternes (see below)

1/2 t. Dill, dried (only for fusion version)

Olive Oil, Butter, Salt, Pepper

Swiss Cheese (for classic version only)

ADDITIONAL NOTES

For my Russian fusion version you need shitake mushrooms, otherwise champignons. For the finishing wine, use a quality sweet Sherry for the fusion version, or a Sauternes for the classic version. Chateau d'Yquem is the ideal choice if you have the budget.

Gnocchi
with Sage and Brown Butter

400g (14 oz) Potatoes (see notes below)
22g (3/4 oz) Salt
Thyme, fresh
75g (2.6 oz) Flour
 * or 45g Flour and 45g Potato Starch (see notes below)
Sage, fresh
Butter

ADDITIONAL NOTES

Do not use Russet potatoes. I know that they are frequently suggested. Just don't. Use Kennebec or Red Gold potatoes.
If you are going to eat the gnocchi right away, use straight flour. For storage in a restaurant setting, use the mixture of flour and potato starch. They will be gummy for the first few hours, but the next day they won't, and the ones made with straight flour will not be nearly as good on prolonged storage.

Dim Sum Fried Shrimp

45g (1 1/2 oz) Rice Flour

45g (1 1/2 oz) Potato Starch

15g (1/2 oz) Regular Flour

2 t Baking Powder

1 t Salt

1/2 t Turmeric (optional)

2 Egg Whites

30g (1 oz) Potato, cooked

Sparkling Water

ADDITIONAL NOTES

This same technique of using cooked potato in the batter works beautifully on onion rings, too.

There are two main problems with this recipe for the home kitchen. First, the cooked shrimp have a very short time period in which they should be consumed for maximum enjoyment. Basically fry them and eat them the moment they are cool enough to put in your mouth. This is a problem for serving a family who want to eat together and have their food put down on a plate in front of them. It just doesn't work for that. The second problem is that the oil will become saturated with water, and no longer able to produce perfectly crisp shrimp if you have a small home-type deep fryer. Don't expect to be able to make more than 6 shrimp per liter of oil in your fryer at the most. That is, if your fryer's capacity is two liters, you won't be able to cook more than 12 shrimp before the oil will have to be changed for optimum results, and you might not even get that many out if you are dragging extra batter into the fryer with each shrimp you cook. In short, these are absolutely delicious - the best fried shrimp you can eat - but they come with a price.

Wild Duck Leg
Deboned and Stuffed

2 Duck Quarters 200-250g (7-8 oz) each

30g (1 oz) Nut Oil (preferably walnut)

30g (1 oz) Walnuts, shelled in large pieces

60g (2 oz) Onion

1 t each fresh Sage and Thyme

1 clove Garlic

1 Egg Yolk

1 T Breadcrumbs

Sugar, Salt, Pepper

ORANGE SAUCE

200ml (7 oz) Orange Juice

100ml Duck Stock

  * or substitute chicken stock

30ml (1 oz) Cider Vinegar

30g (1 oz) Dark Brown Sugar

1/2 small Onion

3 Cloves (the spice)

1/4 t. White Peppercorns, whole

1 Bay Leaf

ADDITIONAL NOTES

It is best to purchase whole ducks and do the butchery yourself.
Then you will have the bones to make the stock, as well as having
duck breasts you can cook separately. If you are using wild
(hunted) ducks, then you will need the breast meat to stuff the legs
with, because wild ducks are much leaner than domestic ones.

Deboning and Stuffing
Chicken Legs

2 Chicken Quarters (leg and thigh)

45g (1 1/2 oz) Butter

60g (2 oz) Onion

30g (1 oz) Celery

30g (1 oz) Carrot

1 clove Garlic

45ml (1 1/2 oz) Sherry, Madeira, or White Wine

90ml (3 oz) Chicken Stock

1 t Thyme, freshly picked leaves

1/2 t White Pepper, ground

1/4 - 1/2 t Cayenne

1 Egg Yolk

* Black Truffles, or Truffle Oil (optional)

ADDITIONAL NOTES

This is a great dish for impressing guests. It really isn't as difficult to make as it might seem, once you do it a couple of times.

Naturally the filling can be anything you like, but I suggest keeping it chicken-based, or it becomes strange. When you cut into chicken, you don't want to taste beef or fish. However, you can make this into a Thai style dish by using a filling that includes shrimp and rice noodles, then breading the chicken before you deep fry it. I will be making a video showing this in the near future.

Korean BBQ Salmon

60-90g Salmon trimmings
45ml (1 1/2 oz) Peanut Oil, or substitute vegetable oil
1 t Mustard Seeds
15g (1/2 oz) Ginger, grated
15g (1/2 oz) Garlic
20g (3/4 oz) Scallions
60g (2 oz) Tomato
3/4 t Thyme, dried (or sprigs of fresh thyme)
1/2 to 3/4 t Sichuan Peppercorns, whole
2 T Honey
1 T Lime Juice, fresh
60ml (2 oz) Bae Gochu Sigcho (see index)
1 t White Miso, or substitute soy sauce
1 t Sesame Oil, dark
1 t Sriracha sauce (optional)
1 t Scallions, minced
Red Chili Pepper, a few thin slices

ADDITIONAL NOTES

Miso paste comes in a range of colors and qualities. High quality white miso is what you need here. Don't substitute another type, and don't use cheap miso. This is especially difficult advice to follow if you are in Russia, where finding miso of any color and any quality is nearly impossible, but I developed this dish back when I was in Los Angeles with many large Asian grocery stores available.

Belgian Mussels Roasted in Purée

400g (14 oz) Potatoes, cooked

30g (1 oz) Blue Cheese (see video)

30g (1 oz) Sour Cream

1 Egg, whole

1/2 t Baking Soda

2 t Baking Powder

16-20 Mussels with shells (previously frozen is fine)

Scallions (for plating)

ADDITIONAL NOTES

If you can get frozen New Zealand Green-lipped mussels on the half shell, this becomes an extremely easy recipe, and you can prepare trays of these ahead of time, ready to pop in the oven for banquets or other occasions.

Don't use a strongly flavored blue cheese. It should be subtle.

Also, you can pump up the flavor and the visual presentation by drizzling a contrasting color sauce over the top. That can be anything from a bright green garlic and herb oil, to a spicy red chili aioli. If you are serving a lot, you can make up trays with different sauces over the top, too. This is a fundamental strategy in banquet presentations - use sauces to create the illusion of more variety, because sauces are a lot easier to make than complete dishes.

Monte Cristo Sandwich

Ham, thinly sliced deli type - or turkey, but the original is ham
Swiss Cheese - or Jack, but the original is Swiss
Onion Jam (optional - recipe is included in the video)
Bread, slightly stale

BATTER
45g (1 1/2 oz) Rice Flour
45g (1 1/2 oz) Potato Starch
15g (1/2 oz) Regular Flour
2 t Baking Powder
1 t Salt
1/2 t Turmeric (optional)
2 Egg Whites
30g (1 oz) Potato, cooked
Sparkling Water

ONION JAM
150g (5 oz) Onions
1 T Sugar
90ml (3 oz) Beef Stock, or Veal Stock
30ml (1 oz) Madeira, or good sherry

ADDITIONAL NOTES
The purpose of the cooked potato in the batter is to get a crisp and
delicate texture in the batter. It is one of those commercial food
science tricks that is seldom heard. This also works very well for
making onion rings.

Tunisian Smoked Lamb Kebab
with Cured Lemon

700g (1 1/2 lbs) Lamb Shoulder

1 Lemon, large + 1 T Lemon Juice

2 t Coriander Seeds (in all)

2 t Black Peppercorns (in all)

2 Bay Leaves

3 Dried Red Chilies

1 t Oregano

1/2 t Fenugreek

1/4 t Cloves (the spice)

1 cup (approximately) Coarse Salt

60g (2 oz) Onions

22g (3/4 oz) Garlic

1 T Ketchup

400g (14 oz) Potatoes

Cilantro, fresh

Mint, ideally fresh, but dry is okay

Harissa (as a condiment)

* or substitute a mixture of Ketchup and Georgian Adjika Spice Paste, which I personally prefer.

ADDITIONAL NOTES

Replace the ketchup with harissa, if you don't mind the extra heat and want a better flavor.

Serve this with hummus (roasted garlic and chickpea purée).

Ratatouille Tarts

Eggplant, 3mm slices
Zucchini, 2mm slices
Orange Bell Pepper
Tomato
Garlic
Basil, fresh
Oregano flowers, or fresh

PASTRY
60g (2 oz) Potato, fully cooked
60g (2 oz) Onion, chopped
45g (1 1/2 oz) Sour Cream
45g (1 1/2 oz) Flour
2 Eggs, whole + 1 Egg Yolk
2 Garlic cloves
200ml (7 oz) Olive Oil (for frying)
Scallions for plating (optional)

ADDITIONAL NOTES
The balance of this dish is important. The pastry element is strong, so you need to have enough vegetables stuffing it so that they dominate instead. Be careful not to let the vegetables get oily, or it will taste greasy. Finally, don't forget about the seasoning. The most common mistake restaurant cooks have made on this is not seasoning it enough. There are a lot of vegetables and pastry here, so it needs salt and pepper.

Chicken Livers
with Shallot Croutons, Lardons and Garlic Dressing

Chicken Livers
100g (3 1/2 oz) Bacon, cubed
1 additional Egg, whole
Cherry Tomatoes
Mixed Lettuces

LOAF

140g (5 oz) Shallots, or onion
2 Eggs, whole
30g (1 oz) Cream
60g (2 oz) Butter, melted (in all)
1/2 t Baking Soda
3/4 t Baking Powder
150g (5.3 oz) Flour
1/2 t Cumin, ground
1/4 t Cayenne

DRESSING

Use either a dressing of your own choice, or make a creamy garlic dressing with crushed fresh garlic, mayonnaise, olive oil, lemon juice and salt

ADDITIONAL NOTES

The most important (and difficult) part of this recipe is frying the croutons that you make so that they are crisp and delicious without being burned. Practice on a few first and expect a learning curve.

Croque Madame

18g (2/3 oz) Butter

1 T Flour

90ml (3 oz) Milk or light cream

Nutmeg, grated

White Pepper, ground

Lemon Juice, fresh (see video)

2 Eggs, whole

4 slices Bread

2 slices Canadian Bacon or ham

* 2 slices Swiss Cheese (optional)

Additional melted butter

ADDITIONAL NOTES

Personally I like a lot of lemon juice in the sauce, as well as some dry mustard. It isn't traditional, and it isn't everyone's taste - but try experimenting and see what you think.

This same lemon bechamel works very nicely as an alternative to Hollandaise in many dishes, especially Eggs Benedict.

Four Pigs Hash
Cooking with Leftovers #1

Scraps of different types of pork, as shown

Onions, or shallots

Celery Leaves, or celery (see video)

Red Chili Pepper (scraped and seeded)

Potato

Herbs, dried or fresh (especially bay & thyme)

Demi-glace, or beef stock (see video)

Egg (yolk only)

Black Pepper, freshly ground

ADDITIONAL NOTES

This same approach works very nicely with poultry by combining chicken, turkey, duck and turkey bacon. In that case, swap out the beef stock for chicken stock, naturally.

If you want to make it more Tex-Mex in flavor, use a Jalapeño chili pepper instead of the red one. It's up to you as to whether or not to scrape the seeds out, of course.

If you want to bring this up to the level of a five star hotel, then use confit duck, lightly smoked goose sausage, and goose or duck liver. In this case leave out the chili pepper completely, but add white pepper as well as black pepper. Goose sausage is available online, or if you are ambitious, you can always make your own.

Meat and Potato Casserole
Cooking with Leftovers #2

500g (1 lb) Potatoes

350g (3/4 lb) Meat, assorted - cooked and/or raw

350g (3/4 lb) Vegetables (with some fresh herbs, if available)

1 Onion (plus a few cloves of garlic, if you want)

1 Egg, whole

2 T Mayonnaise

1/2 t Cayenne (plus some fresh ground black pepper)

2 T Melted Butter

ADDITIONAL NOTES

This is a dish that really extends the life of scraps, because after you recook it, you can save this for several days and reheat portions as you need it. So, in all, the meat you started with could last you nearly two weeks counting from the time you bought it, which makes this approach especially useful if you live alone and only have time to cook occassionally.

Demi-Glace

2.5kg (5 1/2 lbs) Veal and/or Beef Bones

300g (10 1/2 oz) Onions

300g (10 1/2 oz) Tomatoes

160g (5 1/2 oz) Celery

160g (5 1/2 oz) Carrots

2 T Parsley, fresh

* 2-3 Garlic cloves (optional)

1 1/2 t Thyme, dried

1/2 to 3/4 t Black Peppercorns, whole

6 Cloves (the spice, not garlic)

1 t Coarse Salt

ADDITIONAL NOTES

In case this wasn't made clear in the video, this is not the traditional Demi-glace of Escoffier's era. This is a more efficient modern restaurant version - and it will produce a *better* result in the final dish. I say that as someone who grew up making this the traditional way hundreds of times, and working as the Saucier in a well regarded French restaurant. The principle difference is that there is no flour in this sauce. Modern fine cuisine relies on reductions, not starch for thickening.

If you want this to be very clear, then warm it and squeeze it through layers of cheesecloth over a sieve. For most applications, it won't matter at all. If you don't want to bother with the messy cheesecloth approach, you can get it fairly clear just by passing it through a China cap sieve (chinois) a couple of times. I rarely bother with either method, since the final sauce being made is usually sieved anyway.

Chana Masala
Swiss Version of the Indian Chickpea Dish

240g (8 oz) Chickpeas, canned

90g (3 oz) Onion, sliced

30g (1 oz) Clarified Butter, or ghee

1/2 - 3/4 t Cumin Seeds

90g (3 oz) Puréed Tomatoes (Pasata)

1 1/2 t Ginger, grated

2-3 cloves Garlic, minced

1/2 to 1 Green Chili Pepper

1 t Tamarind Paste (Blue Dragon brand, ideally)

300ml (10 oz) Chicken Broth

1 T Curry Powder, Madras

1/2 t Garam Masala (see index)

1/4-3/4 t Cayenne Pepper

Cilantro, fresh

Lime, fresh juice

1/2 t Fenugreek Leaves, dried (optional - see video)

ADDITIONAL NOTES

This can be turned into a dip for chips and crackers by puréeing with yogurt, which is also a way of using up leftovers. If you don't care about authenticity at all, then you can use sour cream or mayonnaise to blend it up with.

Pollo Mexicano

500-600g (1 1/4 lb) Chicken Thighs, boneless skin-on

250g (9 oz) Onion

250g (9 oz) Tomatoes, peeled fresh (see video)

2 Green Chilies (ideally Jalapeño), diced

1 head (about 12 cloves) Garlic, chopped coarsely

1/4 C chopped Cilantro, leaves and stems

2-3 t (10-15ml) Liquid Smoke

Jack Cheese (or cheddar, if you prefer)

Sour Cream

Scallions

2 1/2 t Cumin seeds

2 t Oregano, dried

1 t Black Peppercorns

1 t Paprika

3/4 t Thyme

1/2 t Cinnamon

2 t Salt

ADDITIONAL NOTES

Some prefer this without the skin, and it still comes out fine.
Serve with wedges of fresh lime.

Indonesiian Sweet and Sour
Deep Fried Fish

480g (17 oz) Fish, mild flavor such as cod

3 T Flour

3/4 t Turmeric

3/4 t Cayenne

3/4 t Ginger, ground

1/4 t Black Cumin Seeds (Nigella)

Lime or Lemon Juice

200ml (6.7 oz) Cider Vinegar

100g (3.5 oz) Sugar

1 - 2 t Tamarind Paste

1 Star Anise, whole

1/2 t Ground White Pepper

2 Dried Sweet Chilies (see video and index of this book)

2-4 Dried Hot Chilies

85g (3 oz) Onion, coarsely chopped

110g (4 oz) Red Bell Pepper

110g (4 oz) Tomato

30g (1 oz) Roasted Bay Shrimp (see video)

1 t Ginger, freshly grated

1 T Garlic, chopped

ADDITIONAL NOTES

Like all battered and deep-fried foods, be aware that putting the
sauce on top will turn the coating mushy reasonably soon. There
are chemical additives that can prevent this, but these industrial
agents are not for sale to individual consumers. If your deep fried
food stands up to sauce, now you know what is in it.

Sardinian Chicken
Stuffed with Chicken Liver and Eggs

1.8kg (4 lb) Chicken, whole free range

300g (10.5 oz) Chicken Livers, cleaned

3 Eggs, hard boiled and shelled

1 Egg, raw

45g (1.5 oz) Breadcrumbs

22g (3/4 oz) Sundried Tomatoes, minced

2 T (5 g) Parsley, freshly minced

* 10 Juniper Berries (optional)

8-10 Bay Leaves

100g (3.5 oz) Herbs, fresh - assorted

1/2 t Black Pepper, finely ground

1/4 t Saffron - or a bit more if you like

ADDITIONAL NOTES

I have two personal problems with this dish. The first is that the taste is very rustic and simple, which I realize is well regarded in that part of the world, but if you are looking for something to light up your mouth with fireworks, this isn't it. Second, it is virtually impossible to plate it attractively. So why did I choose to make a video of this? Also two reasons. First, because it shows an interesting technique - boiling a stuffed chicken. That's a useful idea, though not (in my opinion) with this particular stuffing. Second, because I had received several requests for an authentic dish from Sardinia, and I do try to honor such requests. I plan to come back to this technique again in the future and make it into something more exciting - but for all the negative things I have said, it is still a satisfying rustic dish that can be part of a large family meal.

Italian Fennel in Cream

5 parts Fennel

3 parts Light Cream (20% fat)

1-2 parts Parmigiano-Reggiano, freshly grated

For each 200g (7 oz) Fennel add:

1 Bay Leaf

1 Garlic cloves

Fennel fronds or parsley for garnish

ADDITIONAL NOTES

This dish *really* shines if you shave some white truffles over the top.

Although this is intended as a side dish, you can pair it with pasta and turn it into a meal by itself. If you have leftovers, slice them up and put them in an omelette with some crisp bacon on the side for a great breakfast.

Index

D

E

F

CPSIA information can be obtained
at www.ICGtesting.com
Printed in the USA
BVHW03s1024220918
528244BV00001B/43/P

9 781934 939987